August Strindberg's

MISS JULIE

A STUDY

August Strindberg's

MISS JULIE

A STUDY

NANDITA SINHA

asia book club

an international publishing house

Published by
Asia Book Club
C 3/1, Janakpuri
New Delhi 110 058
Ph. 9818755529
Email: asiabookclub@gmail.com
Website: www.asiabookclub.com
ISBN: 81-7851-026-X

Printed at Chaman Offset Press, New Delhi 110 002

Contents

Chapter I

Some Significant Movements in Modern Drama

Realism

Both Realism and Naturalism were movements that emerged from the series of massive political and social changes that transformed the western world beginning with the Enlightenment, the 18th century historical intellectual movement that advocated rationality in all spheres of knowledge, and the Industrial Revolution which brought about scientific and industrial advances. The spread of rational philosophy paved the way for a reaction against romanticism. Realism as a movement attempted to describe life without idealization or romantic subjectivity, emphasizing an objective presentation of contemporary life, giving importance to surface details and focusing on the everyday life and common conduct of middle class individuals. The emotional and intuitive were pushed to the background.

Realism developed along with modern science in its emphasis on observation, accurate recording and theorizing about natural phenomena. It also developed along with ideas of social justice, looking at the evils in society and seeking reform.

Realism was influenced by the thinking of August Comte (1798-1857) who developed the theory of Positivism which recognized only natural phenomena or facts that are objectively observable and the doctrine of Materialism which maintained that the facts of the universe could be described in physical terms and explained by the properties of matter and energy. All knowledge was thought to be derived from sensory experience and everything derived from metaphysics, theology or the realm of the speculative was rejected.

Two other thinkers, Charles Darwin and Karl Marx heavily influenced the views and values adopted by the Realists. Darwin in his *The Origin of Species* (1859) stated that the species change over time due to the process of adaptation and applied the scientific method to biology. He set out his laws of natural selection, survival of the fittest, the evolution of all biological life and the essential unity of all living beings through evolutionary descent. This implied that people were controlled by heredity and environment, behaviour was beyond human control and that humanity was a natural object just like any other. An extreme version of his ideas demarcated those fit to prosper and live from those condemned by 'nature' to die, because they are not 'fit' to live. Karl Marx in his *Communist Manifesto* (1848) stated that history is the story of the control by various classes of the economic means of production and as long as the upper classes control the means of production, the poor will be deprived of power and crushed.

Realism's origins were in France and the father of literary realism is Honore de Balzac (1799-1850) who in his *Comedie Humaine* (1842) systematically described the France of his time from the lowest thief or prostitute to the highest aristocrat or political leader. He framed his work as an almost scientific classification of human types, comparable to zoological varieties among lower animals. Gustave Flaubert in 1857 produced his seminal work *Madame Bovary* from which later literary realism was to flow. Flaubert affirmed that the writer must describe what he detests with utter accuracy and heroic honesty

The works of these writers set the foundation for the main tenets of the movement—art must depict truthfully the real, physical world. Truth can be attained only through direct observation; only contemporary life and manners can be observed directly and the observer must strive to be as impersonal as a scientist.

Realism in fiction meant novels with reliable narrators, dealing with contemporary social and political problems, narrative authority and reliability, a contemporary setting, recognizable characters, representative locations, ordinary speech.

While the old fiction depicted a make-believe world of romantic adventure and love intrigues, the new fiction centred itself in a world of hard work and suffering humanity, life in the raw. Often, however, it fell into the danger of an undue emphasis on the sordid and seamy side of life, a piling up of its ugliness and beastliness.

Realist plays were a reaction to the melodramas, comic operas and vaudevilles that dominated the theatre from 1859 to 1900. This kind of drama depended upon trite situations and stock characters, with morality drawn in extremes of black and white, where virtue was always rewarded just as vice was always punished. It indulged in set formulas, reinforced by a great deal of rhetorical speech with hardly any concern for the psychology of character and motivation.

The theme of realism in the theatre was direct observation of human behaviour and likeness to life. The plays became a laboratory for the nature of relationships. Equally importantly, the on-stage environment, the dress code, and language was part of the audience's own environment. It was distinctly human beings feeling and acting in places and with objects about which there could be no mistake; the characters were specifically located and specifically occupied with material reality in a material world. With the director Stanislavsky came the idea of "inner realism" in character creation, training the actor to react as he would if he were actually the character rather than the player. Its basis is the idea of "truth," of fidelity to life which is the over-all principle of realism.

The style of acting introduced by realism not only called for natural behaviour and speech but for the observation of what is called the 'fourth wall' convention—the assumption that the open space formed by the proscenium arch is the fourth wall of the room. Consequently the actor was not supposed to see the audience, the playgoers are simply not supposed to exist. In fourth wall staging, every effort was made to disguise the fact that the stage is a platform for players and to create the illusion that it is a true environment and separate from and independent of the auditorium. The actor could turn his back on the audience whenever the action required.

Realism appeared in Russia even earlier than in France and it was even more uncompromising. Ivan Turgenev's *A Month in the Country* (1850) is representative. Even though he gives a faithful representation of the daily life of a country estate, the domestic detail is a foil that serves to reveal the inner turmoil of his characters. Anton Chekhov (1860-1908) sets each of his plays—*The Sea-Gull* (1896), *Uncle Vanya* (1899), *The Three Sisters* (1901), *The Cherry Orchard* (1904)—in rural Russia, depicting the monotonous and frustrating life of the land-owning class. All the characters aspire to a better life, but none knows how or has the initiative to achieve his goals. Chekhov's plays are built upon subtle detail, which require attention to nuance if the pattern behind the surface is to become clear. Gradually a unified mood and a complete simple action emerge. Chekhov's realism consisted in complete objectivity. "Freedom from . . . falsehood" was his aim. I have not introduced a single villain nor an angel. . . . I accused nobody, justified nobody."[1] It is the life below the apparently placid surface that interested him, instead of a strong plot or striking events, his emphasis was on the psychological motivations of characters.

But the father of modern realist drama is Henrik Ibsen (1828-1906). With plays like *A Doll's House* (1879), *Ghosts* (1881) and *An Enemy of the People* (1882), Ibsen established his reputation as a radical thinker and controversial dramatist. His is the drama of ideas. The basic theme in his plays is constant—the struggle for integrity, the conflict between duty to oneself and duty to others. Much of Ibsen's work contributed to the development of realism in the theatre. He discarded asides, soliloquies and other non-realistic devices and was careful to motivate all exposition. All scenes are causally related and lead logically to the denouement. Dialogue, settings, costumes and events are selected for their ability to reveal character and milieu and are clearly described in stage directions. Each role is conceived as a personality whose behaviour is attributed to heredity or environment. Internal psychological motivation is given even greater emphasis than external visual detail. In these ways Ibsen provided a model for writers of the realistic school. Most dramatists after Ibsen were influenced by his conviction that drama should be a source of insights, a creator of discussion, a conveyor of ideas, something more than mere entertainment. He gave playwrights a new vision of their role.[2]

Realism in England had its champion in George Bernard Shaw through his concern for ideas and social problems, and in American drama, the names of Clifford Odets, William Saroyan, and more importantly, Arthur Miller and Tennessee Williams are associated with this tradition.

Naturalism

Naturalism as a philosophical doctrine denies the existence of metaphysical or supernatural phenomena and concentrates solely on the material world. In literature it is an approach that proceeds from an objective analysis of reality in terms of natural forces—heredity and environment as determinants of man's fate. This doctrine was based on Darwin's *The Origin of Species* (1859) which, as we have already seen, set forth two main tenets: (1) that all forms of life have developed gradually from a common ancestry and (2) that the evolution of species is explained by the 'survival of the fittest'. These theories had several important implications. First, they make heredity and environment the causes of everything man is or does. Second, since behaviour is determined by factors largely beyond his control, no individual can be truly held responsible for what he does. If blame is to be assigned, it must go to a society that has allowed undesirable factors to operate. Third, man is reduced to the status of a natural object. Before the 19th century, man had been set apart from the rest of creation as superior to it. Now he lost his privileged status and became merely another object for study and control. (Brockett, 468-69)

Naturalism as a literary movement first appeared in France in the 1870s. Its origins can be traced to the publication of *Germaine Lacerteux* by Jules and Edmond Goncourt in 1865. But it was another Frenchman, Emile Zola who formulated a manifesto for Naturalism. His creed was consonant with 19th century worship of mechanistic science as the key to all truth. He especially reflected the advances made in physiology by Claude Bernard (1813-1878), the founder of experimental medicine. He wrote *Le Roman Experimentale* in 1880. Drawing continual parallels between his own aims and the aim of experimental medicine, Zola casts the novelist as a pathologist and suggests that he study the effects of heredity and environment on character with scientific objectivity.

In drama, Zola found classical tragedy and romantic drama absorbed in idealization and abstraction: "Never the thoroughgoing analysis of an organism . . . never a character whose muscles and brain function as in nature." Hence for him the history of Naturalism could be summed up in the gradual substitution of 'physiological man' for 'metaphysical man.' His desire was to probe beneath the surface and reveal what lay within. His success lay in liberating the stage from romantic "heroic" drama. Zola fought fiercely to liberate the theatre from dead formulas and he demanded the right to tell the truth with pitiless candour.

The strictly naturalistic view was mechanistic, physiological, and deterministic. Man is seen as puppet and victim of these inexorable forces. Most naturalists demonstrated a concern with the animal or irrational motivations of human behaviour, sometimes manifested in connection with sexuality and violence. Individuals were seen as simply the product of heredity and a particular environment, motivated by inner instinctual drives and pressured by the forces of society without. They had little will or responsibility for what took place in their lives. Thoughts, desires, intentions, feelings and actions all arise on their own without the benefit of a supervisory self, and they are all products of a physical system, the brain and the body. Naturalists are anti-Romantic in their rejection of the self-defining hero who transcends his background. History shapes the protagonists rather than being shaped by them. This leads to an overwhelming sense of doom, culminating in a final catastrophe.

Naturalism affected performance and presentation in the theatre. It insisted upon "nature as opposed to an abstract ideal of beauty" and 'speech as opposed to declamation.'

By stressing photographic detail in scene design, costume and acting technique, it attempted to abolish the artificial theatrical techniques prominent in 19th century theatre. The underlying justification for this concern with the elements of external verisimilitude was not a simplistic preoccupation with these details in themselves but rather a conviction that they helped to establish an inner authenticity. It was in such an atmosphere that Zola's demand that the new actor must "not play but live before the audience" could best be satisfied.[3]

Dramatic form also changed in response to the new ideological changes. The drama of adventure and intrigue was replaced by drama shaped and expressed as experience. Form became organic. The plays invariably manifested characteristics of spontaneity and disregard for mere theatrical effect. Plot was always the servant, never the master of psychological or social reality

An important part of Naturalistic theatre was the concept of setting as environment, a manifestation of the conditions of life with which the characters in the play must struggle. The stage thus acquired individuality and meaning as a controlling factor. Similarly acting methods reflected the new shape of the drama. Edvard Brandes, one of the famous directors of this period wrote: "Acting is above all the depiction of human beings. . . . We do not go to see a tragedy in order to enjoy a sonorous voice, watch pleasing gestures and tableaux, or admire a pretty face. The pleasure we seek to experience is the essence of the personality, to observe the human soul in its inmost intricacies laid bare before us." (Marker, 163-64)

The movement was most clearly associated with the Theatre Libre (1887) of Andre Antoine, with the Freie Buhne (1889) of Otto Brahm and with the Moscow Art Theatre (1898) founded under the direction of Stanislavsky. Notable naturalistic dramatists include Becque, Brieux, Hauptmann and Gorky.

Henri Becque (1837-990) is one of the best examples of the naturalistic playwright in France and his play *Les Corbeaux* has been described as the Bible of French naturalism. He rebelled against the norms of the well-made play where the audience was always prepared for any development in the action. His plays are full of abrupt transitions and sudden events, and are totally devoid of sentimental glamour, because that is how life is in reality

Hauptmann's play *Before Dawn* (1889) showed the influence of the theories of Zola and inaugurated the naturalistic movement in the German theatre. His other realistic plays include the famous tragedy of the working class *The Weavers* (1892). The play deals with the economic situation of the cottage weavers of Silesia and the depression of their wages caused by the introduction of machinery is the precipitating force. Their conflict with an employer who is himself a victim of economic forces unleashed by the industrial revolution has tragic dimensions.

Maxim Gorky is considered the father of Soviet literature and the founder of the doctrine of socialist realism. His play *The Lower Depths* (1902), a study of the wretched lives of derelicts, remains a classic. It consists mainly of the scattered gossip of unfortunates huddled in a lodging house kept by a receiver of stolen goods—an artless picture of the underworld as the author knew from painful experience. There is no evidence of structure, no central figure, no dramatic action, and there is a most extraordinary collection of the tragic riff-raff of humanity. The play exemplifies his opinion that the characters of drama should act independently of the volition of the dramatist in accordance with the law of their individual natures and social environment, follow the inspiration of their own destiny and act in harmony with their own contradictory natures, interests and passions. Gorky's intimate experience of the outcasts of society is presented with stark realism. As one of the characters in the play says: "Life is not tragic throughout, it flows softly, monotonously by, like a great muddy river, and while you are watching it flowing your eyes become weary, your head becomes dull, and you don't even want to think what the stream is flowing for. Life crushes us without noise, without screams or tears and nobody notices it."

An important concern with the naturalists was the influence of environment and in some naturalist plays it assumes even the role of a concentrated antagonist. Chekhov, for example, noted the corrosive effect of provincial life in several of his plays. Environment is so important a factor in *The Three Sisters* that Fate is identified with stagnation in a provincial town. And Ibsen pitted the reformer Dr. Stockman against an entire Norwegian town in *An Enemy of the People*. Dr. Stockman wants to expose the contaminated condition of the waters of a bathing resort. The town, which derives considerable income from those who come to the resort in search of health, suppresses the idealist.

Strict naturalism did not work in the theatre because the dramatist's use of the materials of social reality was interpretative, whereas Zola's "scientific" programme for naturalism demanded absolute objectivity and clinical detachment. The doctrinaire naturalists soon alienated the public with the grossness of their plays and the tawdriness of their stage productions. Their plays became nothing more than 'photography' depicting life in its crudeness and ugliness, its formlessness and colourlessness. The strict application of the standards of naturalism led to a flood of depictions of degradation, disease and sexual license in theatrical circles after 1880.

The naturalistic play had freed the stage of the formulas and fictions. It had pointed the way to a more faithful depiction of life. But in doing so, it allowed entry to many playwrights who were merely academic, who took credit to themselves that they were offering *tranches de vie*, fragments of reality: that they were eschewing asides, avoiding coincidences and artificial complications in plot, when in fact, they were imaginatively arid. Naturalism was responsible to a considerable extent for the anti-realist reaction represented by the 'symbolist' plays of Maeterlinck.[4]

Symbolism

Symbolism bridged the transition from Realism to Modernism. The Symbolist movement began in France with the publication of a manifesto in 1886 by Jean Moreas, in which he announced that Symbolism was hostile to "plain meanings, declamations, false sentimentality and matter-of-fact descriptions," and that its aim was 'to clothe the Ideal in a perceptible form.' French Symbolism, therefore, may be seen as a reaction against Realism and Naturalism, and the dominance of positivism, which emphasized rational thought, objectivity and scientific method. Instead of an objective reality, the Symbolists favoured spirituality, the imagination and dreams. Their intention was to capture the absolute through indirect methods—allusions, symbols, myths and legends They held the idea that truth or reality could be found in the unconscious. Hence their style was highly metaphorical and suggestive.

The symbolists were greatly influenced by the poetry of Charles Baudelaire, whose *Les Fleurs du mal* (*Flowers of Evil*, 1857) embodied many of their literary ideals. Baudelaire's doctrine was "synaesthesia"—the mixing of the senses. He also developed a theory of "correspondences" or relationships among objects of sense and spiritual reality. Other important figures were the poets Stephane Mallarme, Paul Verlaine, and Arthur Rimbaud. Mallarme was of the opinion that "poetry should not inform, but suggest and evoke; not name things, but create their atmosphere." For the symbolists, music was the supreme art, because it eliminated the denotative restriction of words and had infinite meanings. These ideas of musical effect, indefiniteness and suggestiveness were major shaping influences on modern poetry.

The influence also passed over into drama. Many writers around this time felt that theatre had lost its meaning and had become only a form of entertainment. Paralleling movements in art and poetry, they used symbol, abstraction and ritual in an attempt to revitalize the theatre. The originator of many anti-realist ideas was the German opera composer Richard Wagner. Wagner felt that art should create myths and that the dramatist should portray an ideal world in which the audience shared a communal experience, as the ancients had done. He sought to depict the "soul-state" of inner being. He proposed what he called "Gesamtkunstwerk," the "total art work" in which all dramatic elements are unified under the control of a single artistic creator.

The Symbolist movement in France was the first to adopt Wagner's ideas. The symbolists called for "detheatricalizing" the theatre, stripping away all that was extraneous and replacing it with spirituality that was to come from the text and the acting, creating a mood that was slow and dream-like. (See http://literal 1no4.tripod.com/dramahistory.html)

In drama, as in poetry, the symbolists were concerned with the internal life of the individual. They focused on subjective mental impressions, delicate emotions and moods, spiritual and irrational states of mind and even psychic phenomena. Strong symbolist elements can be found in the plays of Chekhov and the late plays of Ibsen and Strindberg. Symbolism also influenced the Swiss theorist Adolphe Appia and the English designer Edward Gordon Craig, whose innovations shaped much of twentieth century scenic and lighting design. Maurice Maeterlinck was the foremost playwright of the symbolist movement and the greatest Belgian playwright of the nineteenth and twentieth centuries. His masterpiece, and the greatest works of symbolist theatre are *Pelleas and Melisande*, which was produced at the Theatre de l'Oeuvre in 1892 and *The Blue Bird* (1909), an enormously popular story from which is derived the phrase "the blue bird of happiness." Maeterlinck's influence on Strindberg was to be felt in plays such as *Easter* (1901), where the child Eleanora symbolizes the desire of the human spirit to bring happiness to others; and in *The Crown Bride* (1904), where Strindberg spoke of "omitting analyses, questions and viewpoints, seeing only beauty in depiction and mood" (Styan, Vol. 2, 44) The symbolic mode is also used in *A Dream Play* where towards the end, the castle is on fire, yet from the cracks in the earth, grass and weeds poke up, and through the disintegrating brick wall ivy drives its shoots. From out of the fiery building sprouts a giant chrysanthemum. The flower is an affirmation of the blessing of life and growth.

Expressionism

Expressionism arose in Europe in the late nineteenth and early twentieth centuries as a response to the bourgeois complacency that permeated society, its order, efficiency and obsession with social conventions, which often led to a hypocritical attitude towards sex. Increasing mechanization and urbanization of society also contributed to what many sensitive persons saw as an imaginatively arid milieu.

Expressionism originally emerged in the fine arts, initiated by the Paris exhibition of Fauvist painters, at the Salon des Independants in 1901 which included several canvases grouped together under the title "Expressionisme" by the otherwise unknown painter John Auguste Herve. Unlike the Impressionists whose goal was to reproduce the impressions suggested by the surrounding world, expressionism aimed at strongly imposing the artist's own sensibility to the representation. It raises subjective feelings above objective observation. This led to the use of heightened symbolic colours, exaggerated imagery, agitated brush-strokes, disjointed space. There was a tendency to distort reality for raw and powerful emotional effect. Edvard Munch's *The Scream* (1894), a lithograph depicting a figure with a contorted face screaming in horror, epitomized the tone of much expressionist art: "Man screams from the depths of his soul, the whole age becomes one piercing shriek. Art screams too, into the deep darkness, screams for help, for the spirit. That is expressionism," said Austrian author Hermann Bahr.[5] The scream could be said to be the defining image of Expressionism. It was really the desire to capture the essence of life in all its chaos, violence and rage.

Expressionism's roots struck deep in Germany and the defining event was World War I. An important influence was Friedrich Nietzsche's prose poem *Thus Spake Zarathustra* (1885) with its theme of the "New Man," which led to related themes of the "new vision" and the "new society," where spiritual renewal is linked to social regeneration. Art serves the purpose of political idealism. A sense of alienation often goes hand in hand with a search for meaning in life.

The leaders of the movement in drama were Georg Kaiser (*The Burghers of Calais*, 1913, *From Morn to Midnight*, 1916, *Gas*, 1918), Ernst Toller (*Masses and Man*, 1921) and the Czech

Karl Capek (*R.U.R.: Rossum's Universal Robots*, 1921), from which, Styan notes (Vol. 3, 54), the term robot, the Czech word for 'slavery' was coined. These dramatists looked back to Georg Buchner (*Danton's Death*, 1902, *Woyzeck*, 1913) Strindberg and the German actor and dramatist Frank Wedekind (*Spring's Awakening*, 1906, and *The Lulu plays*, 1898,1905) as precursors of their dramaturgical experiments.

Expressionist dramatists tried to convey the dehumanizing effects of 20th century technological society through such devices as minimal scenery, sudden shifts from prose to verse, from objective reality to highly subjective monologue, from conventional dialogue to telegraphic utterance, and characters portrayed as types rather than as individuals. Unnecessary details were eliminated and the characters were often representatives of states of mind or social positions. They used the grotesque to distort reality and present a totally personal viewpoint. The emphasis in many cases was not on visual details but on visionary experiences in an effort to objectify complex psychological states and gain mystical access to permanent values. The intention was to go beyond the logical, rational world to the deeper reaches of the soul. The style was a conjunction of extremes—compression with expansiveness, clipped logicality with hymnic incantation, the concrete with abstraction, the sublime with the prosaic. The settings were often abstract, shadowy and colourless.

Expressionist drama took many directions. It could be the drama of protest where the inner turmoil of the main character is expressed in monologues, broken, incoherent, and illogical. Personal tragedies often end in the destruction of the character. However when the focus is on the state of society, there is often victory of traditional human values over repression and mass production. It could also have religious overtones and cosmic dimensions, where the central character moves in the direction of a revelation or transformation, making crucial decisions as he follows a certain path through life. Hence this drama is centred on the pilgrimage motif and is modelled on the ancient religious model of the stations of the cross.

August Strindberg is often referred to by literary historians as the Father of Expressionism. His post-Inferno period inaugurated his "expressionist" period. *To Damascus I and II*, has a protagonist called the Stranger, who is Everyman, possessing within his character the entire range of human experience, representing Strindberg's conception of Man in combat with his fate and Man in search of himself. His struggles, guilt and atonement are structured in the form of a pilgrimage and everything takes place in an atmosphere of free association that gives a sense of the fluidity of a dream. The play has a circular structure, with the second half of the play mirroring the first, so that it appears to be a journey into the depths of the subconscious and back again. Egil Tornqvist comments: "Presumably for the first time in the history of drama, we are confronted with a play in which an inner reality is consistently dramatized, or better: in which the border between outer and inner reality is blotted out."[6] The dream consciousness reigns supreme. This leads to an intense subjectivity that was to become a vital part of all subsequent Western drama.

Strindberg's most influential expressionist play is *A Dream Play* (1912). In the Preface, he writes that he has tried "to imitate the disconnected but apparently logical form of a dream. . . . Anything can happen; everything is probable and possible. Time and space do not exist; on a slight groundwork of reality, imagination spins and weaves new patterns made up of memories, unrelated fancies, absurdities and improvisations. . . . The characters split, double, redouble, evaporate, condense, scatter, and converge. But one consciousness remains above all of them: the dreamer's." Individual characters become archetypes of the psychological and historical functions through which we define ourselves and are extensions of facets of the dreamer's own self. It is an exploration of the hidden world of the mind and the visual elements assume prominence as images from the realm of dreams. Strindberg's anti-realistic stage directions called for "stylized murals suggesting at the same time space, architecture and landscape." The setting included gigantic brilliantly coloured hollyhocks, a cave with geological formations and green waves, a castle with a flower-bud on the roof which turns into a huge chrysanthemum, a tree which turns into a coat and hat-stand.

Strindberg's "chamber plays" had as their aim "the concept of chamber music transferred to drama," stressing their intimacy, lyricism and simplicity of theme. It was drama in a reduced and concentrated form, consisting of a motif and variations, eliciting in the spectator not so much an intellectual response as a mood. *The Ghost Sonata* was subtitled A Fantasy, and the play is a series of images suggestive of a dream. There is a symbolic quest that takes us through evocative visions of guilt and expiation, of innocence and evil. The house becomes a central symbol, reflecting the evil and moral depravity of its dwellers, who are tormented spiritually and physically by the sins of the past. Sickness and corruption abound. The hallucinatory atmosphere has a mummy emerging from her closet squawking like a parrot; a grotesque ghost supper culminating in a suicide; a Hyacinth Girl, a vision of beauty and love, who turns out to be an emaciated woman, drained of her strength by a vampire cook. The play's deeply pessimistic vision seems to symbolize the "curse" which "lies over the whole of creation, over life itself" and from which the only liberator is death.

Ingmar Bergman, who directed the play, said: "The whole play is a dream—fairly realistic at the beginning, but growing more and more grotesque as the action develops." Hence, he wanted everything in the production to be "immediate, naked, simple." It was drama as subjective, emotional experience. J.L. Styan sums up Strindbergian expressionist drama as one "which made few demands on the conceptual thought of the audience, but through musical form, lyrical and incantatory language, mime and other visual suggestion, pause and silence, and the distortion of time and place, his appeal was to inner experience, unconscious feeling, akin to nightmare" (Vol. 3, p. 38). From his work can be traced a direct line to all that is most "modern" in modern theatre.

References

1. J.L. Styan, *Modern Drama in Theory and Practice* (Cambridge: Cambridge University Press, 1981), Vol. I, p. 83.
2. Oscar G. Brockett, *History of the Theatre* (Allyn and Bacon), p. 468.
3. Frederick J. Marker and Lise Lone Marker, *A History of Scandinavian Theatre* (Cambridge University Press, 1996), p. 163.
4. John Gassner, *Perspectives on Modern Drama and Theatre* (New York: Holt, Rinehart and Winston, 1956), p. 71.
5. See David Galens, ed., *Literary Movements for Students* (Detroit and London: Thomson-Gale, 2002), Vol. 2, p. 892.
6. Qtd. Colin Chambers, ed., *The Continuum Companion to Twentieth Century Theatre* (London and New York: Continuum, 2002), p. 732.

Chapter II

Strindberg and Naturalism

Both as a playwright and as a theorist, Strindberg kept in close touch with the newest developments in theatre and drama, not only to absorb them but to reshape and expand them in his restless search for new forms with which to encompass his extraordinary dramatic imagination and fertile consciousness. Strindberg's interest in a new kind of dramatic form was boosted by what is called the Modern Breakthrough, a period in Scandinavian literature characterized by the prominence of science and positivism in place of the traditional Christian faith, and drawing much of its initial inspiration from the Danish critic Georg Brandes, who emphasized that literature ought to deal with contemporary issues such as class, marriage and sexuality.

This was also the time when Strindberg was strongly influenced by the so-called psychology of suggestion, immersing himself in the theories of Liebeault, Bernheim and others who were investigating such phenomena as hypnotism and mesmerism. He was extremely anxious for his plays to be staged in Paris, where Zola's naturalism was in vogue. At the same time he was trying to establish his Scandinavian Experimental Theatre. These three facts explain why Strindberg precisely at this moment was so concerned with psychological, naturalistic, one act drama. As always he desired to be abreast of the most recent developments, especially when they were related in some way to scientific experimentation.

From the early 1880s he was preoccupied with the emergence of Naturalism and its quest for new formulae in drama. The demand of naturalism that staged events should mirror real ones were eminently fulfilled in the one-act plays he wrote at this time, in the sense that unity of time and place are usually observed—so much so that playing time often precisely corresponds with the scenic time. Strindberg's first 'naturalistic' play *The Father* (1887), uses a single setting, a 24 hour time-span, and a plot revolving around a single conflict—a confrontation between husband and wife over their daughter that soon assumes archetypal proportions. The economy of the dramatic form highlights the psychological dimensions of the conflict, a "battle of brains" which ends tragically. The psychological depths of the question of gender and class are further explored in *Miss Julie* (1888). With its exceptional concentration—the plot time nearly coincides with the performance time of about 90 minutes—and its unflinching investigation into the combination of attraction, repulsion and dependence that ties Julie, the Count's daughter to the valet Jean, the work is probably Strindberg's masterpiece. The naturalistic method is to trace effects to their causes. It takes a dramatic situation, in this case, Julie's aggressively coquettish behaviour towards the servant, his alternations of reluctance and eagerness, leading up to a seduction and then to regrets on both sides and finally to Julie's suicide. Then, while observing the details or outward effects coolly, even scientifically, naturalism traces their causes: Julie's lonely, unnatural upbringing, the struggle for power between her parents, her training at becoming a man-hater, the setting in the servant's quarters which for a time makes Julie feel reckless; the intoxicating scent of flowers and the even more intoxicating wine; the festive atmosphere of Midsummer's Eve, Jean's yearning since childhood to be on par with the upper classes. The analysis builds up to a revelation of painful truths. Strindberg further honed his naturalistic style in a number of one-act plays, including *Creditors* (1889), *The*

Stranger (1888-9), *Pariah* (1889) and *Motherly Love* (1892). Though these plays follow naturalism in their emphasis on the pathological, they depart from its documentary technique to achieve a subjective, emotional tone.

As Marker puts it: "For him 'naturalism' became synonymous with what he described as "the great style, the deep probing of the human soul." He was never convinced by the merely photographic concerns of the movement or by its sometimes exaggerated insistence on the reproduction of the details of surface reality. "If a woman is seduced in a hothouse," he wrote, "it isn't necessary to relate the seduction to all the potted plants you can find there and list them all by name" (197). Though in his dealing with contemporary subjects and with problematic immediate life and also because of the colloquial manner, Strindberg's plays resembled those of the movement's acknowledged leaders, Zola and Hauptmann, the fact is that Strindberg developed his own brand of naturalism by cutting away all the verbiage and incident required for realistic authenticity and concentrating solely on moments of crisis and catastrophe. He called himself a "nyanaturalist," a 'new' one, creating plays of psychic and spiritual warfare, whose apparent intention was to reveal the brutalizing effects of sexual love. The primary emphasis is not on the customary naturalistic interaction between character and a convincingly lifelike environment. It is rather on the battle of the sexes primarily as psychological warfare.

Thus he dissociated himself from the kind of naturalism that focused solely on external and visible phenomena and left little room for the imagination to operate. His powerful vision went far beyond the naturalistic principles of fidelity to social reality and its recording of sociological data. The greater naturalism that he aimed at was that "which seeks out the points where the great battles are fought, which loves to see what you do not see every day, which delights in the struggle between natural forces—whether these forces are called love or hate, rebellious or social instincts—which finds the beautiful or ugly unimportant if only

stincts—which finds the beautiful or ugly unimportant if only it is great" (Marker, 197). The emphasis is on the intensity of the dramatic mood and conflict.

In 1887 Zola wrote to Strindberg: "I demand to know everything about the characters' positions in life so that one can touch and perceive them, sense them in their own atmosphere." In *Miss Julie*, Strindberg followed Zola's dictum and attempted to bring in an unbroken slice of living reality. The audience was allowed to experience the events on stage as though they were actually occurring in real life.

In his famous Preface to *Miss Julie*, Strindberg combined features of the naturalistic aesthetic with ideas that point in a new direction. At the centre of his argument he put the idea of character—what it had meant in the theatre and how he himself conceived of it. He points out that "Character" had become a name for an individual who had stopped growing, stopped developing and thus had become representative for the "bourgeois conception of the immutability of the soul," "a man fixed in a mould." A person who goes on developing and does not sail a predictable course is defined as "characterless" because he is "difficult to catch, classify and keep tabs on." But Strindberg is aware of the complexity of motives—biological, environmental, hereditary—that underlie behaviour and for him psychology added depth in the creation of what he called a "soul-complex." He writes: "In real life an action—and this, by the way, is a somewhat new discovery—is generally caused by a whole series of motives, more or less fundamental, but as a rule the spectator chooses just one of these. . . . I have drawn my people as split and vacillating, a mixture of the old and new. . . . My soul (or characters) are agglomerations of past and present cultures, scraps from books and newspapers, fragments of humanity, torn shreds of once-fine clothing that has become rags, in just the way that a human soul is patched together."

Strindberg's second argument is related to plot and motivation. In a way his views were a reaction to the iron-clad formulas of the well made play, the lack of subtlety in its pattern of exposition, complication, and denouement with the predictable defeat of the villain and the triumph of the hero. Strindberg was familiar with the dramatized version of Zola's *Therese Raquin* and though he saw that Zola had to a certain extent probed into Therese's mind and focused upon her motives, he felt that it was not enough. "In the pangs of conscience of criminals," he wrote, "[Zola] sees merely an expression of disrupted social harmony, the results of habit and inherited ideas." To Strindberg "true" naturalism meant truth to nature. So Strindberg determined to have his own plays deal in fundamental truths, like those of the sexual relationship, the psychological conflict of wills and the bearing of the past on the present (Styan, Vol. I, 38), but always focusing on what he called "multiplicity of motives."

Strindberg also amplified his own conception of proper performance style, the changes he had made in the structure and aesthetic patterns of dialogue: "I have departed somewhat from tradition by not making my characters catechists who ask stupid questions in order to elicit a smart reply. I have avoided the symmetrical, mathematical constructions of French dialogue, and let people's minds work irregularly, as they do in real life where, during a conversation, no topic is drained to the dregs, and one mind finds in another a chance cog to engage in. So too the dialogue wanders, gathering in the opening scenes material which is later picked up, worked over, repeated, expounded and developed like the theme in a musical composition." The aim is thus the naturalist's concern with faithfulness to observed life, mirroring the randomness and casualness of everyday conversation.

The theatrical reform that he advocated in his Preface carried over to his staging of *Miss Julie*. As Marker describes it: "To enable the audience to experience the events on stage as though they were actually occurring in life, no disruption was allowed to disturb the intense focus on the fateful confrontation between Julie and the valet Jean. The customary intermission was eliminated by the playwright, lest it break spell of the "author-mesmerist's suggestive influence." To strengthen the illusion of reality, the large kitchen in which the action is set was meant to be fully three-dimensional in order to eliminate the strain of having "to believe in painted pots and pans." At the same time, however, the setting was conceived impressionistically, with the use of asymmetry that stimulated the imagination by leading the eye of the spectator "off into an unknown perspective." In proposing the elimination of footlights and heavy make-up and the introduction of strong side-lighting to accentuate eye and facial (i.e. psychological) expressiveness, Strindberg advocated a close-up of subtler reactions that were 'mirrored in the face rather than in gesture and sound.' Following Antoine's lead, he called for the actor to disregard the audience seated beyond the invisible fourth wall and to perform within, rather than in front of, the setting. In this way each scene would be played 'at whatever spot the situation might demand.' 'I do not dream that I shall ever see the fullback of an actor through the whole of an important scene,' he writes, 'but I do fervently wish that vital scenes should not be played opposite the prompter's box as though they were duets milking applause.' (201)

Though Strindberg thought of himself (in the period 1884-1892) as a naturalist, citing his "innovations" such as multiplicity of motives, the concept of 'characterless' character, the realistic production values and the Darwinian survival-of-the-fittest in his preface to *Miss Julie*, there were several features in the works of this period that undercut the naturalist position that he professed to adopt, in particular his obsession with the sex war and his pro-male stance. As his interests and attitudes changed in his post-Inferno years, so did his belief in the efficacy of Naturalism as a style for the modern consciousness, leading him to scornfully classify this genre as a symptom of "the contemporary materialistic striving after faithfulness to reality."[1] His search now was for spiritual truths and his increasing need to strip the soul naked led him to adopt the methods of symbolism and expressionism.

Reference

1. Robert Brustein, "Male and Female in August Strindberg," *Modern Drama: Essays in Criticism*, ed. Travis Bogard and William Oliver (New York: Oxford University Press, 1965), p. 342.

Chapter III

Strindberg: Life and Works

August Strindberg was born on January 22, 1849 in the Riddarholm district of Stockholm. His father, Carl Oscar Strindberg, was a shipping agent with pretensions to aristocratic lineage. His mother, Ulrika Eleanor Norling was a tailor's daughter who had been a domestic servant before becoming Carl Oscar's mistress and then his wife. August was the fourth of eleven children, the first to be born in wedlock, a fact that would haunt him in his later years with doubts about his paternity. It also resulted in an obsessive concern with the question of class. As a child he was precocious and hypersensitive. Strindberg's early life was spent in poverty in the aftermath of his father's bankruptcy. He was very attached to his mother and her death when he was thirteen years old shattered him. To make matters worse, his father remarried within a year, this time to his housekeeper, arousing intense hostility in the mind of the young boy.

In 1867, Strindberg entered the University of Uppsala, but academic formalism was not to his liking and he left without a degree. He tried teaching, acting and then playwriting, producing two comedies and a verse tragedy. Returning to the University in 1870, he helped found the Runa Society, a student group devoted to Nordic folklore and literary pursuits.

Strindberg began his career as a playwright profoundly influenced by the romantic theatre's preoccupation with history and folklore, a tradition still in full bloom in Sweden. He had modest success with his play *I Rom*, depicting the youthful struggles of the great Danish sculptor Thorvaldsen to follow his artistic calling. It was followed by another one-actor, *The Outlaw*, a saga play set in twelfth century Iceland on the theme of the conflict between Christianity and heathenish.

At the age of twenty-three, he began work on his first truly major play, *Master Olof* (1876), a play about the Swedish reformer Olaus Petri, who by becoming a tool for other men's purposes ends as an unheroic figure and a traitor to his cause. The play was so powerful and unconventional that he could not find anybody willing to stage it and was forced to revise it (When it was eventually produced in December 1881, it marked the emergence of Strindberg as a major dramatist). Moody, brooding and difficult, incapable of concentrating on any job for long, he was a misery to himself and others. He threw up theatre and took up journalism. Then went back to acting and again back to journalism. In 1874, he became an assistant librarian at the Royal Library in Stockholm, a position which he retained for eight years and which gave him for the first time economic stability and status.

Strindberg was a strong-willed young man, with a keen sense of sexual superiority and intellectual power. He was also restless and unable to make any lasting friendships. He was twenty-six when he fell properly in love. She was Siri von Essen, a member of the Swedish aristocracy and the wife of Baron Carl Gustav Wrangel, and an aspiring actress. In 1876, Siri divorced her husband following an attempted suicide by Strindberg and in 1877, she married the man who had been a frequent guest at her home. The marriage lasted until 1891. Their first child, born two months after the wedding, did not live and Strindberg never lost the sense of guilt he felt over the death of his first born, though three children followed.

A period of happiness resulted in a successful production of *Master Olof* and a modest output of fiction, of which *The Red*

Room and *The New Kingdom*, both savagely satirical stories of contemporary Sweden caused a furore. This was followed by another collection of stories *Married* (1884) which advocated an egalitarian relationship between men and women, though maintaining a traditional view of the sex roles. The second volume, composed in 1885, was obviously written by a man suffering under very serious mental disturbances. He arrives at the conclusion that all of womankind, and especially the 'emancipated' woman have banded in league against him. It was a bitter volume, presenting marriage as a form of mental and emotional extortion, in which women, by nature parasites, have the upper hand. He and the publisher were charged with blasphemy, though they were acquitted after a trial.

By this time his marriage with Siri had turned sour. Although there were times when he loved her devotedly he was continually torn by jealousy, hatred and every emotion of an excited and unbalanced mind. It could not have been easy for Siri to cope, especially as she felt that she had abandoned a promising career as an actress to lead an unsettled life with a restless and increasingly paranoid husband. To add to their problems was the failure of a play—*Sir Bengt's Wife* (1882)—that Strindberg wrote in response to Ibsen's *A Doll's House*. It is the first play in which the woman question comes to the fore in Strindberg's dramatic imagination. Unlike Nora in Ibsen's play, Margit is reunited with her husband at the end, as the warfare of the sexes is overcome by the bonds of a love stronger than either rational logic or individual will.

Lucky Per's Journey (1882) employs a vaguely medieval setting and a fairy tale atmosphere that echoes the great works of Scandinavian romanticism, not least the stories and plays of Hans Christian Anderson. As young Per wanders about the world in search of happiness, he realizes that his dream of gold and honour and power brings with it bitter disillusionment. The play proved to be one of Strindberg's most resounding successes. The misty dream-like transitions in the play, its replacement of the logic of reality by the fairy-tale's logic of fantasy and its magic realism all point to the 'dream plays' of Strindberg's maturity.

This was the beginning of what has been called the "wander years." From 1883 through 1891, the couple travelled extensively, settling at various times in France, Switzerland, Bavaria and in 1889, again in Sweden. Their marital and financial problems worsened. This was the time that Strindberg wrote a brilliant autobiographical novel *The Madman's Defence*, containing incidents and character relationships that he would use again in his naturalistic plays.

He also enlarged the scope of his interests to include philosophy and psychology. He corresponded with Nietzsche, and became a follower of Emile Zola's naturalistic movement, producing three plays which mirrored his own profound anxieties—*The Father* (1887), *Comrades*, *Miss Julie* and *Creditors* (1888), the last a psychological masterpiece which he himself considered his best work. This is a one-act play depicting the betrayal and destruction of the husband Adolf by his scheming wife Tekla and her lover. The ending shows the wife collapsing on his body, begging his forgiveness as she swears she loves him. These plays established Strindberg's reputation as a major dramatist. *The Father* and *Miss Julie* were staged by Andre Antoine, who helped Strindberg realize the dramatic possibilities of the one-act play. In fact, all three plays were designed to be performed by a small company with a minimum of technical and financial resources. (Strindberg described *Creditors* as "a naturalistic tragedy, even better than Miss Julie, with three characters, a table and two chairs and no sunrise").

Strindberg's stormy marriage to Siri ended in 1891. Although there were times when he had loved her devotedly he had been continually torn by jealousy, hatred and suspicion. There followed a period of acute poverty and mental turmoil. He moved to Berlin where he met and married Frida Uhl, an Austrian journalist, another disaster which ended in divorce in 1897.

The next few years are known to us as his "Inferno crisis," a time when he lived as a recluse, went through psychotic experiences, believing himself persecuted by corrective spirits he called the Powers, engaged in chemical experiments, took up alchemy, delved in the occult, hypnotism and black magic, and often landed up in prison or hospital. It was a state of near-insanity.

He emerged from this crisis a self-styled religious man, whom readings of Pythagoras, Origen, Schopenhauer and especially the work of the Swedish scientist and religious thinker Emmanuel Swedenborg (1688-1772), (whose notions of correspondences and transformations in particular appealed to him) had convinced that earthly life was "a half-reality, a bad dream." From then on, his work began to have a mystical and religious cast, in which he grappled with the condition of mankind in a metaphysical context.

A period of intense activity from 1898 to 1909 produced thirty-six plays. There were historical dramas—*The Volsunga Saga* (1899), *Gustav Vasa* (1899) *Gustav Adolf* (1900) and *Erik XIV*. These were followed by *Charles XII* (1902), *Queen Christina* (1901), *Gustave III* (1902). In all these plays, the historical background is less important than the inner lives of the characters, their passions and weaknesses. Thus the central character in *Gustav Vasa* is portrayed as a powerful ruler who nevertheless wavers at crucial moments. Strindberg remarked: "Even in the historical dramas, the purely human is of major interest, and history the background: the inner struggle of souls awakens more sympathy than the combat of soldiers or the storming of walls; love and hate, and torn family ties, more than treaties and speeches from the throne." (Marker, 214)

Then there are plays in which he continued to work out his own inner conflicts. The parent-child conflict is explored in

Motherlove (1894), where a rapacious former prostitute refuses to allow her daughter to see her natural father even though she is being supported financially by the girl. Later, he would write *Crime and Crime* (1900) which deals with the death of his first child and the sense of guilt it left him with. Sexual conflict is the theme of plays like *The Stranger* (1889), dealing with the question of marital infidelity from a most unique angle and *The Dance of Death* (1900), where the focus is on a marital conflict in which a couple who have been married for twenty-five years live in inescapable proximity to each other, torture each other, but are unable to leave each other until the woman succeeds in killing the man, not with a knife or poison but with sheer malice of mind and despite this concludes that she must have loved as much as she hated him. The mounting symbolic significance of the setting combines with insistent repetition to create a hallucinatory world suggesting the proximity of death. *The Virgin Bride* (1901) draws on Swedish folklore and traditional music to present the plight of a young bride who has concealed the fact that she has had a baby so that she can remain entitled to wear the parish-wedding crown. The play traces her path from deceit to truth-telling and eventual religious conviction. The role of suffering is given a central ethical function.

A trilogy *To Damascus* (1898-1904) became the first of what Strindberg was to call "dream plays." It is also a 'pilgrimage' play, The central motif is Saul's conversion and transformation into St. Paul on the road to Damascus. The themes revolve around temptation, sin, guilt and the search for salvation, atonement and reconciliation. The central character The Stranger, is in a way Strindberg himself. He is Everyman, possessing within himself he entire range of human experience and representing Strindberg's conception of man in combat with his fate and man in search of himself. The Lady is a composite portrait of his three wives (by now he had again married, this time a young Norwegian actress Harriet Bosse, despite nearly thirty years' difference in their ages; she left him in 1903, after only two years of marriage, unable to cope with his excessive jealousy and protectiveness). The play is full of references and allusions to events in his own life, including frightening spiritual and psychic experiences that take him to the brink of insanity. The atmosphere of free association gives the work the fluidity appropriate to dream. The play is a landmark in twentieth century drama because it creates a dream world that is both fantastical and meaningful, thus foreshadowing later developments in drama like surrealism, expressionism and theatre of the absurd.

For his next play, *A Dream Play* (1902), Strindberg wrote a preface that documents his thinking about the new shape of drama as he envisaged it:

> In this dream play, as in his former dream play *To Damascus*, the Author has sought to reproduce the disconnected but apparently logical form of a dream. Anything can happen; everything is possible and probable. Time and space do not exist; on a slight groundwork of reality, imagination spins and weaves new patterns made up of memories, experiences, unfettered fancies, absurdities and improvisations.
>
> The characters are split, double and multiply; they evaporate, crystallize, scatter and converge; but a single consciousness holds sway over them all—that of the dreamer.

With plays such as these, Strindberg began to gradually reject older stage conventions as inadequate means of expressing the mystic and visionary qualities that he came to regard as the essential texture of reality. The unconscious and the irrational are now intrinsic elements embedded in the play. *A Dream Play* like the earlier *To Damascus* is an attempt to present "the disconnected but apparently logical form of a dream." It fuses together the themes that had obsessed Strindberg from the very beginning—the pattern of sin, guilt and atonement; the meaning of suffering and the core of love-hate in all relationships between men and women. The daughter of Indra comes down to earth, marries, bears a child and learns what it is to love and suffer as a human. Her conclusion is "mankind is to be pitied," for suffering is inherent to the human condition and rises from the inevitable conflict between the flesh and the spirit. The play presents a powerful, though ambiguous series of hallucinatory images and nightmarish fantasies that mirror the patterns of dream. It is an attempt to bridge the gap between the conscious and the unconscious, with the belief that it is through the unconscious that we can most truly confront ourselves and our God

Three intensely active years followed the period of Strindberg's 'dream' plays and produced what are known as the "chamber plays," all written in 1907. Strindberg had all along wished to establish a small intimate theatre where he could stage his own plays in accordance with his innovative ideas about acting and stage design. He drew inspiration from the Chamber theatre (Kammerspiele) that Max Reinhardt had opened in Berlin. A young actor-producer named Augustus Falk came forward with a practical scheme, and on November 1907 the Intima Teatern, seating 161 persons, was opened in Stockholm. Strindberg had ready a cycle of four plays, and his goal, he said, was the concept of chamber music transferred to drama. It was to be, he wrote, "intimate in form, a simple theme treated with thoroughness, few characters, vast perspectives, freely imaginative. . . . Simple but not too simple, no huge apparatus, no minor parts." (Marker, 217). The strongest influence on the style of these chamber plays was probably his own occultist experiences as well as his loathing of existence. The themes of guilt and expiation predominate.

In *Storm Weather* (1907), the first of the chamber plays, the atmospheric evocation of the twilight of summer and of life centres on memories of an unhappy past and the reality of an equally unhappy present. In *The Burnt House* (1907), the Stranger arrives to expose the buried truths of relationships within the lives of families, relentlessly stripping away the illusions of the past and exposing evil and hypocrisy, so that the world is seen as a tissue of lies and cheating in which death comes as the settling of accounts. The play is full of allusions to the Garden, the Tree of Knowledge and the loss of childhood innocence. *The Pelican* (1907) is a violent play of brutal divisions between a mother, son, daughter and son-in-law, bringing to the fore themes of limitless avarice and exploitation in the most sacred of relationships, an intense drama of human anguish and purgation. The title comes from the myth of the bird which is supposed to give its own blood to its starving young, but in the play the reality is horrifyingly different. The best known of these chamber plays, however, is *The Ghost Sonata* (1908), has a hallucinatory clarity that is almost surrealistic, focussing on the universality and inescapability of guilt, which bears down on the 'innocent' and 'sinful' alike. The dominant consciousness in the play is a student named Arkenholz who undertakes a dream journey, a mythic quest which takes him to characters who embody cruelty, madness, evil and death. Strindberg parodies and inverts the fairy-tale pattern of the return-to-Paradise. Here guilt is ever-present, innocence non-existent or 'doomed', suffering for no fault of its own, the world is one of 'illusion, guilt, suffering and death . . . endless change, disappointment and pain.' As the Student says: "The curse lies over the whole of creation, over life itself." Mays comments: "Out of his own conflict between paradise and the fallen world, fairy tale and reality, Strindberg made stunning drama."[1]

In 1908, Srindberg moved to his last home The Blue Tower, which now houses the Strindberg museum. His last play was called *The Great Highway*, another dream play. He also wrote articles in newspapers on religion, politics and literature which led to a press feud which lasted two years. He died of stomach cancer in 1912 while living in virtual isolation. His funeral was attended by crowds of admirers. Though he did not have the honour of receiving the Nobel Prize, he was awarded the Anti-

Nobel prize—fifty thousand crowns through public subscription—two months before his death

Strindberg ranks among the most influential of modern dramatists. His vast range of work touched upon almost all modern dramatic styles, from naturalism and symbolism, to expressionism and even a kind of surrealism. Practically all innovative writers and painters of the twentieth century came under his sway, were unable to escape his legacy whether or not they knew his work at first hand. The Russia-born Arthur Adamov said, "It was Strindberg, or more exactly *A Dream Play*, that incited me to write for the theatre." In his journal, Franz Kafka wrote: "I feel better because I have read Strindberg. I don't read him in order to read him, but to press myself against his breast." The image of trying to remain close to Strindberg's heart signifies a filial warmth towards Strindberg. So does Bertolt Brecht's characterizing of him as "one of the great educators of modern Europe." Eugene O'Neill once said he wished that "immortality were a fact, for then some day I would meet Strindberg"[2] and called him "the most modern of moderns, the greatest interpreter in the theatre of the characteristic spiritual conflicts which constitute the drama—the blood—of our lives today."[3]

References

1. Milton A. Mays, "Strindberg's Ghost Sonata: Parodied Fairy Tale on Original Sin," *Modern Drama*, 10 (2), September 1967, pp.189-194.
2. *European Writers, Volume 7, The Romantic Century* (New York: Charles Scribner's, 1985), p. 1732.
3. *Twentieth Century Literary Criticism* (Thomson Gale, 1978), p. 443.

Chapter IV

Miss Julie: An Overview

Miss Julie, A Naturalistic Tragedy in One Act, as Strindberg titled it, was published in 1888 and produced in 1889. The play was a by-product of his marriage with Siri von Essen, who was also the first to act the decadent young countess. The play was originally conceived for performance by a small experimental theatre, but when Strindberg finally did manage to set up his own Scandinavian Experimental Theatre in Copenhagen, the venture survived only a week. His troupe then set up quarters in Dagmar Theatre, one of Copenhagen's leading private theatres, but one day before the opening of *Miss Julie*, the play was banned by the public censor because of its daring subject matter. Finally, the premiere took place at a private showing before 150 spectators in a makeshift theatre in the student union of the University of Copenhagen (Marker, 202-3). The next performance came only in 1893, when Otto Brahm staged it at his Freie Buhne in Berlin. The first Swedish production was in 1904 in a private performance at Uppsala University, and it was as late as 1949 that the full Swedish text was staged at the Royal Dramatic Theatre in Stockholm (Styan, I, 39). One of Strindberg's most popular works, it was made into a ballet in 1950, an opera in 1966 and filmed in 1951 and 1999, the recent production being directed by Mike Figgis.

The play is set in the kitchen of the Count's mansion, on Midsummer's Eve, a festive occasion. There is music and danc-

cook is working at the stove when the valet Jean enters carrying the Count's riding boots. He informs her that he has just returned from dropping the Count off at the station and that he has seen the Count's daughter Miss Julie dancing with the gamekeeper. Both feel that she is "crazy" and Kristin replies that Miss Julie's behaviour has been particularly bad ever since her engagement was broken off. Jean tells Kristin the real cause of the breakup. He has surreptitiously watched Julie making her fiancée jump over her riding whip, "training" him, and hitting him with it each time he jumped. The third time, the man took the whip away from her, broke it and left her. Kristin pampers Jean, stroking his hair tenderly and gives him a slice from the joint of meat in the frying pan. Jean refuses her offer of beer, bringing out a bottle of expensive wine instead. He points out that, like her mother before her, who was most at home in the kitchen and the cowsheds and yet would not drive with only one horse, who would have dirty cuffs and yet have coronets on her buttons, Miss Julie has no respect for herself or her position.

Julie enters the kitchen to collect the brew for her dog, Diana, who has "got herself into trouble" with a mongrel, something Julie will not put up with, Kristin tells Jean. Despite Jean's servile but impertinent remonstrations, Julie coquettishly leads him back to the dance, while Kristin suppresses her resentment with a sanctimonious "I know my place, my lady." Julie appears to be in full control of the situation: "I'm the mistress here," she says. Jean returns shortly after, certain that she is really mad to be behaving in this way, and as he fondly puts his arm round her waist, Kristin explains that she's always queer at "these times" of the month. Julie enters and chides Jean for leaving her. She tells him to take off his livery, because it is a holiday. As he moves away, Julie asks Kristin whether Jean is her fiancée. When Jean returns Julie compliments him in French. He replies in French, telling her that he had learnt the language when he was a waiter in one of the best hotels in Switzerland.

Meanwhile, Kristin has dropped off to sleep. Julie asks for a drink and Jean slyly tells her that there is only beer. Eager to please him, Julie replies that her tastes are simple and she prefers beer to wine. They drink together, she makes him drink her health and then tells him to kiss her shoe. Jean is uncomfortable lest someone come in and see servant and mistress together, a lady drinking with a man. But Julie is unconcerned. She continues her flirtation, inviting him to come out and pick lilacs with her. Jean is initially reluctant but as Julie opens up and tells him her dreams, he too is led, in his half-euphoric state, to confess to her his childhood miseries and aspirations.

Julie's dream is one of degradation. She is on top of a pillar, longing to descend to the ground, but she does not have the courage to jump. Yet, she says, "I know if I *were* down, I should want to go deeper and deeper into the earth."

Jean's dream is one of aspiration. He is lying under a tree in a thick and dark wood; he wants to climb to the top of the tree to look out over the brightly-lit landscape and rob a bird's nest of its golden eggs. Despite persistent climbing, however, he never arrives at the first branch, much less the top.

Finding that Jean has a speck of dust in his eye, Julie tries to get it out with her handkerchief, all the while acting in a very provocative manner. Jean warns her that it is "dangerous to play with fire," that "there's inflammable stuff about," and that he has too much "self-respect" to act as a playmate for her.

He describes his wretched existence in poverty and squalor and how the Count's park appeared like the Garden of Eden to him. One day, while weeding the onion beds, he landed up in the gentry's outhouse (the Turkish pavilion). To avoid discovery he left through the privy and sewer, only to surface to spy on Julie, in pink dress and white stockings, standing in the rose garden. He tells her: "you represented to me the utter hopelessness of ever rising out of the class where I was born." But, he confesses, since then, he has learnt a great deal about the upper classes and

"Perhaps, after all, there isn't as much difference as they think between your class and mine."

Jean's uneasiness persists. Foremost in his mind are his reputation and the fact that being thrown out without a reference would jeopardize his ambition to "get on in this world." He almost begs her to go to bed and leave him alone, but Julie would rather he row her out on the lake to watch the sun rise.

The peasants are heard singing a bawdy song and as they come towards the kitchen, Jean retreats with Julie to his room to escape discovery. Their off-stage sexual consummation is signalled onstage by a crescendo of the sounds of the revelling peasants. When Julie and Jean return, there is a visible change in their relationship. Jean has coarsened visibly and is now the one in control. He suggests that she run away with him to Switzerland where he will start a hotel. He has no money and he tells Julie that if she wants to be his partner she must bring the capital, callously insinuating that money is really what matters to him. As long as they are in the house there will be barriers between them—the past and the Count. In fact, the very sight of his gloves and his boots, standing stiff and proud is enough to make him feel small and servile. In another country, he says, these class notions can be forgotten; he will make a fortune, go to Romania and buy himself a title.

Just as Julie had flaunted her superiority before the sexual act, so Jean flaunts his now, ruthlessly abusing her dignity by refusing to be tender. Breaking into hysterical remorse, for she realizes that her position is now that of a servant's mistress, Julie wonders what drew her to him—was it the intoxication of the festival night? "The attraction of the weak to the strong, the ones on the decline to the ones rising." She calls on God to end her misery, but Jean taunts her crudely, telling her that his story about wanting to die for her was mere make-believe. As she sees Jean taking out the bottle of wine, she accuses him of stealing from her father's cellar and calls him a thief, a menial and a lackey. He responds by calling her a menial's whore and a lackey's tart.

He tramples on all her illusions about love by gloating on the fact that this affair has been a learning experience for him, a discovery that what had so far dazzled him in the upper classes was "only tinsel, and the fine complexion's powder, and the polished nails are black-edged-and the handkerchief may be dirty in spite of its perfume." Yet any sense of triumph or defeat is negated by the enormity of their situation. The two plan their departure to Switzerland, Jean to start his hotel, Julie to escape her shame. Though she loathes him, she cannot leave and insists on talking of her family's sordid past, the struggle for power between her mother and father, with each taking revenge on the other in cunning and ruthless ways, and her upbringing as a man-hater, in itself the source of psychological conflict, because of a love-hate relationship with her father. "But occasionally—when my weakness comes over me—oh, the shame of it!"

Julie still harbours notions of love and romance, "By Lake Como, where the sun's always shining, and the oranges shine on the trees, and the laurels have fresh green leaves at Christmastime." But Jean brutally cuts her off with an account of the sordid realities—Lake Como is a "rainy hole," full of quarrelling tourists. He makes it clear that he holds the upper hand in every respect, demolishing all Julie's pretensions to rank and class by pointing out that her family has been founded by a miller, who let the king sleep with his wife one night in the Danish wars. "My stock's better than yours—no one in my family ever committed arson" and in a display of supreme male arrogance: "I haven't got that kind of ancestor, but I can found a family myself." Now Jean regards himself as an equal, if not the superior—he can patronize Julie in her predicament, "With us, love's just a game—something to do in our time off; we haven't got all day and night for it, like you. I believe you are ill—yes, that's it, you must be ill."

As the sordid horror of her act presses down on Julie, she is confused and disoriented, begging Jean to "order" her, because she can neither act nor think on her own. Jean orders her to get dressed, get some money and come down. Kristin enters the kitchen dressed to go to church. She is surprised to see Jean looking "ready to drop," notices the two glasses and puts two and two together. Her horrified reaction to his daring act is that it is wicked and disgusting; and unbelievable, too, because "she [Julie] wanted to have poor Diana shot for going with the porter's mongrel." She takes refuge in a sanctimonious morality that bases itself on class consciousness—it would be "degrading" for her to continue to work in a household where "you can't respect your betters," because "class is class all the same." Jean plays for time.

The sun has risen and is slanting through the window. Julie re-appears in travelling clothes, a smudge of dirt on her face, carrying her pet bird in a cage. Asserting his masculine dominance, Jean refuses to let Julie take the bird along, decapitating it on the chopping block. A hysterical Julie loses all self-control and expresses a brutal death-wish for the entire male sex. She raves about her hatred for men and gloats as she envisions her father's stroke upon discovering her doings.

Yet when Kristin returns, Julie throws herself at her, appealing to her for sympathy and understanding as a woman, and begging her to join them. She also resorts to a kind of bribery, painting in glowing terms the pleasures of travelling and seeing the world. And in a desperate kind of capitulation to Jean's proletarian ambitions, she speaks of running a hotel, even fudging the bills, using the same expression that Jean had used, "There's a life for you!"

Kristin's faith in grace, forgiveness of sins and redemption of the Last who will become the First, hypocritically sanctimonious though it is (especially her moralizing comment on how it is "easier for a camel to pass through a needle's eye, than for a rich man to enter the Kingdom of Heaven"), gives Julie a moment of hope amidst her shattered fantasies, hope that is destroyed when Kristin self-righteously leaves for church, after a parting shot about giving instructions to lock up the stables, that tells Julie of the impossibility of any escape.

She picks up the razor with which Jean has been shaving and urges him to seduce her into killing herself. In a moment of self-awareness, she sees that she is the one who will have to bear the blame and suffer the consequences. Her moral victory is affirmed, and as the count's bell rings unexpectedly for Jean, he suddenly becomes totally servile and bereft of will power, ready to take up his role as a menial. Julie begs him to save her honour, save her name, order her to cut her throat, to hypnotize her so that she will obey him. She enters a trance-like state and experiences a hallucinatory moment when the room feels full of smoke and Jean appears like an iron furnace like a man dressed in black with a tall hat, and eyes glowing like coals. When the bell rings again, Jean quails. But finally he turns to her: "It's horrible! But it's the only way to end it!—Go." Holding the razor he puts into her hand, Julie walks out to the barn.

Chapter V

The Preface to *Miss Julie*

Strindberg wrote the preface to *Miss Julie* after completing the play and it is now considered a landmark document of the tenets of naturalism in theatre. His dramatic method was experimental but always designed with a specific moral and social agenda in mind. Hence the preface represents both an ideological as well as an artistic manifesto. Its importance can be gauged by the fact that it was read to the audience on the occasion of the performance of *Miss Julie* at Berlin's famous avant-garde theatre, the Freie Buhne, by one of its founders and directors, the noted journalist and critic, Paul Schlenther. And copies of a French translation were distributed at the Theatre Libre in Paris when Antoine staged this play. (Gassner, 258)

Strindberg begins by envisioning the playwright as "a lay preacher peddling the ideas of his time in popular form." He refers to what he calls a "major crisis" in the theatre, and European drama in general, the fact that "pure, disinterested appreciation has become impossible," and bemoans the lack of new forms to fit the new contents.

Strindberg is fundamentally concerned with the ethical and intellectual response his work evokes in an audience. He insists that he has "not tried to do anything new—for that one can never do—but merely to modernize the form so as to meet the demands which may, I think be made on this art today." He also claims to avoid the controversial issues of his times, and to concentrate on those of "lasting interest"—"questions of social climbing or falling, of higher or lower, better or worse, of man and woman." This he sees as a subject for tragedy, arousing the tragic emotions of pity and fear.

At the same time, he is careful to point out that these feelings may be relative only, "since the alternation of rising and falling is one of life's principal charms"; just as the big eats the small, it also happens that "the bee kills the lion or at least drives it mad." Thus Strindberg, giving expression to his proletarian bias, looks forward to a time when "we shall be happy and relieved to see the national parks cleared of ancient rotting trees which have stood too long in the way of others equally entitled to a period of growth—as relieved as we are when an incurable invalid dies."

Strindberg next comments on the popular rejection of the tragic. For him, what is conventionally termed "the joy of life" is equivalent to the farcical. In contrast, he says, "I myself find the joy of life in its strong and cruel struggles, and my pleasure in learning, in adding to my knowledge." Thus Strindberg invites an audience to regard his play as an opportunity to witness the painful but ultimately rewarding process of discovery and change, in short, to learn.

A further innovation, he says, relates to plot. His is neither simple, nor is its point of view single, because in real life, "an action . . . is generally caused by a whole series of motives, more or less fundamental." As regards his treatment of theme, it is neither exclusively physiological nor psychological, because the emphasis is on the "multiplicity of motives." Thus he replaces the older cause and effect pattern with a depiction of the unconscious drives and desires which shape human actions.

Strindberg then goes on to speak of his "characterless" characters. "Character," he says, had become a term for an automaton, one whose nature had become fixed, who had ceased to grow. The term 'characterless' became a derogatory term for one who tended to develop and grow, because he was so "hard to catch, classify and keep track of." Strindberg himself advocates what he calls "the richness of the soul-complex," where vice has a reverse side very much like virtue, and where characters are "vacillating, disintegrated, a blend of old and new." "My souls (characters)," he goes on to say, "are conglomerations of past and present stages of civilization, bits from books and newspapers, scraps of humanity, rags and tatters of fine clothing, patched together as in the human soul." This is a classic declaration of early modernism, that human nature is elusive, contradictory, indeterminate, ambivalent, capable of feeling both love and hatred towards the same person, as Strindberg's personal experience evinced.

A considerable part of the Preface is devoted to amplifying Strindberg's theory of dramaturgy. He rejects the "symmetrical, mathematical construction of French dialogue" in favour of a kind of dialogue which mirrors the actual patterns of conversation, which generally meanders along in fits and starts, thus "gathering in the opening scenes material which is later picked up, worked over, repeated, expounded and developed like the theme of a musical composition."

Strindberg thinks of the dramatist as a "hypnotist" throwing over his audience an aura of illusion. So that this effect remains undisturbed, he abolishes the division of the play into acts, in order to maintain the "illusion," at the same time giving relief to the play-goers through devices like monologue, mime and ballet, all having their origins in classical tragedy. Monologue can be made to be natural provided the correct motives are established and Strindberg believes that it may even encourage improvisation, thus taking a step forward to a 'productive' art form. He replaces crowd scenes by the ballet.

In fact, as Styan notes, "All Strindberg's requirements for the intense concentration of the audience during the performance clearly indicate his idea of dramatic illusion. His audience was to be completely convinced of the reality of the world of the stage, and transported wholly into its sphere of influence." (Vol. 1, 43)

As regards scenery, Strindberg takes his inspiration from impressionist painting, "its asymmetry and its economy." He decides to show only part of the room where the action takes place so as to give the imagination scope to visualize the rest. He avoids "over-decoration of his single set," and rejects "painted pots and pans."

In proposing the elimination of footlights and heavy make-up and the introduction of strong side-lighting to accentuate eye and facial (i.e. psychological) expressiveness, a small stage and a small playhouse, Strindberg advocated the close-up drama of subtler reactions that were "mirrored in the face rather than in gesture and sound." Following Antoine's lead, he called for the actor to disregard the audience seated beyond the invisible fourth wall and to perform within, rather than in front of, the setting. In this way, each scene would be played "at whatever spot the situation might demand"

Apart from the dramaturgical arguments that he advances, Strindberg uses his preface to explicate his characters and define the "multiplicity" of their motives. He identifies the factors responsible for Julie's tragic fate, including her parents's and her fiancé's characters, her upbringing, the mood of the Midsummer Eve festival, the urgency of the sexually aroused Jean, Julie's "monthly indisposition," chance and other biological and environmental conditions, which makes her a "half-woman," a "man-hater," a type that "thrusts itself forward," "implies degeneration," producing misery and bringing forth off-spring "to whom life is torture." Strindberg's misogyny breaks out in his statement: "fortunately they perish," because their "hopes of catching up with men are shattered."

Paradoxically, he finds this "desperate fight against nature" to be tragic. He sees in it a kind of nobility, a "new nobility of nerve and brain" which incorporates "an innate or acquired sense of honour," a very "beautiful thing," but one which has fatal consequences, since it impels to suicide the nobleman who has done something ignoble and lost his honour. Thus Julie, as victim of "the day's complaisance, of circumstances, of her own defective constitution," is impelled to take vengeance on herself.

Strindberg's analysis of Jean shows a similar identification joined with hostility, representing his lifelong psychic split over the question of class. The portrayal brings in what he calls "a little bit of evolutionary history," i.e. social Darwinism, which proposed that individuals fight for position in society much as animals fight for their survival in the wild and that, in humans as in animals, only the fittest can survive. Jean is the upwardly mobile servant of "dual, indeterminate character, vacillating between love of the heights and hatred of those who have already achieved them." He is both polished and vulgar, having both "the slave's brutality and the master's lack of squeamishness. He is an aristocrat sexually and can dominate Julie because he is a man. Strindberg stresses his virility, his keener senses and his capacity for taking the initiative. He can also lie and manipulate easily, hence he emerges from the battle unscathed. His "slave mentality" makes him "worship" the Count as well fear him, because the count represents the higher class to which he aspires.

Though Strindberg's Preface was written ostensibly to reinforce his ideas about naturalism in the theatre and in his play in particular, he has, in reality, created a disjunction between the theoretical, essentially pragmatic intentions of the preface and the creative intentions in the play. Many of the ideas do not reflect directly upon the actions and strategies in the play. As Gassner notes "the ideal of scientific detachment, or, if you will, impartiality, the cornerstone of naturalistic ideology, is absent, despite attempts at 'naturalness' of speech and external appearance, and the avoidance of romantic fripperies . . . it is dramatic complexity that provides the really valuable naturalistic texture of these plays." (258)

Most important is the breakdown of the borders between the conscious and the unconscious. Far from merely evoking a surface "reality," Strindberg employs symbolic devices which are suggestive of the non-rational aspects of characters and events. Strindberg's naturalism, his new realism about sexuality and class, goes beyond environment and heredity and spills over into expressionism which plunges into the depths of the psyche, where characters verbalize emotions in their quest for an essential identity. In fact, its continued success on the stage lies less in its naturalism than in its blending of naturalism and expressionism. The dreams Jean and Julie recount blend the conscious with the subconscious in an exploration of an elusive truth.

Further, the naturalist belief that individuals had little will or responsibility for their fates is here countered with the idea of existentialist choice. *Miss Julie* is not about characters who are doomed to a fate determined by their peculiar temperaments and upbringing, as the preface would like us to believe. Rather it is a play which shows us two people who move inexorably to their respective fates through actions they take under the influence of a sequence of circumstances at once random and of their own making, and by making choices for which they must ultimately take responsibility. Hence Strindberg's term "naturalistic tragedy" is paradoxical.

Finally, there is the ambivalence towards the characters that goes against the rigid codifications of the naturalist stance, a clear instance of the overlap of personal and artistic consciousness. Brustein sees in this a case of split sympathies. He writes: "Despite his pretence at scientific impartiality, for example, his misogyny is still perfectly clear, for he characterizes Julie as a 'man-hating woman', a type that 'forces itself on others, selling itself for power, medals, recognition, diplomas, as formerly it sold itself for money.' At the same time, though he affects a Darwinistic indifference to the supersession of the 'old warrior nobility' by the new nobility of 'nerve and brain', he admits that the aristocrat's code of honour was 'a very beautiful thing' and that the new man rises in the world only through base and ignoble tactics." (335)

There is no doubt that the Preface is a remarkable document, as much for its originality as for its comprehensiveness. It shows Strindberg trying to give traditional forms a distinctively "modern" shape. Strindberg has managed to find a place in it for everything that was new and controversial, whether in theatre (Antoine), literature (Zola), painting (the impressionists), biology (Darwin), sociology (feminism), psychology (Ribot, Bernheim), politics (the rise of the lower classes) or philosophy (Nietzsche) and to blend these with his own personal predilections.

Chapter VI

A Background to the Play

Strindberg is one of the most subjective of dramatists and his creative brilliance allowed him to use the events of his own life—his childhood, his three marriages and experiences with women, and later his experiences with the occult and the psychic and transform and objectify them into intense dramatic form. As Gilman notes: "What he succeeded in doing—no writer has ever done it more violently—was to place his nature on exhibition, objectifying its contradictions, confusions and ambivalences in the most amazingly varied forms."[1]

The first and greatest of Strindberg's misfortunes was his birth. It led to personal and artistic conflicts that shape his work. His aristocratic leanings inherited from his father clashed with his proletarian background, as the 'son of a servant', and emerged as a lifelong psychic split over the question of class. The psychological dualism also manifested itself in feelings of rebellion as well as submission to a father figure, as well as attitudes to women that veered between the desire to find a mother figure whom he could worship and a simultaneous fascination for the 'emancipated' female whom he could hate.

The other shaping influence was his three failed marriages and his turbulent relationships with the women in his life, so that the theme of the "battle of the sexes" becomes a personal rather than a social one. All his three wives were career women who were attractive, intelligent and ambitious and who refused to take up the role of the simple domestic housewife that Strindberg seemed to have wanted. Always at the back of his mind was the

Madonna-like figure into which he had idealized his dead mother who had never given him the love that he longed for.

This led him to a misogyny that is characterized by a simultaneous idealization and degradation of women. On the one hand he saw the male, strong of mind and heart, but in the generosity of strength guileless and over-trustful; on the other side, the female, weak of body and intellect, but shrewd enough to exploit frailness and contriving by her treacherous cunning to enslave her natural superior. He was a haunted man, distrustful of people and especially of women, and yet he was inexorably drawn to them.

Strindberg's autobiographical novel *The Son of a Servant*, subtitled "The Evolution of a Human Being, 1849-1867" is an important entry point into the mind of this temperamental genius. The fourth of eight children he yearned for more of his mother's time and affection than she could give. He condemns her unjustness, violence and small-mindedness; she is the servant of the book's title. "But since the children received food and comfort from her, they loved her." His relationship with his father was equally ambivalent. He was "a stranger, more an enemy than a friend," and yet he goes on to remark: "that is the thankless position of the father in the family—the provider for all, the enemy of all." The family, he concludes, is the "home of all social evils, a charitable institution for indolent women, a prison workshop for family breadwinners, and a hell for children."

Critics have attributed Strindberg's anti-feminism not only to lack of motherly love, and his hostility towards his stepmother, but also to a greater sociological movement prevalent in the contemporary works of Hartmann, Schopenhauer, Nietzsche—all avidly read by the playwright.

Schopenhauer's writings on women stress her "weaker reasoning powers," the fact that "women remain children all their lives" and that they must attach themselves to some man because "she requires a master." He writes: "Nature has not destined them, as the weaker sex, to be dependent on strength, but on cunning; this is why they are instinctively crafty"; and further, "dissimulation is instinctive in women," and "women, in truth, exist entirely for the propagation of the race; they live more for the species than for the individual." Brustein points out: "it is highly probable that Strindberg read Schopenhauer's *Metaphysics of the Love of the Sexes*, which affirms that sexual attraction is a diabolical invention for the propagation of the race by the 'will of the species . . . ready relentlessly to destroy personal happiness in order to carry out its ends'—and that the satisfaction of this will leaves the love with 'a detested companion for life'." (324)

Nietzsche, too, expresses similar ideas: "One half of mankind is weak, chronically sick, changeable, shifty"; "In woman, a slave and a tyrant have all too long been concealed"; "In a woman's love is injustice and blindness to all that she does not love." (See www.theabsolute.net/misogyny/nietzschewom.html) In fact, Nietzsche, with whom Strindberg became acquainted through his friendship with Georg Brandes, became one of the important influences on the playwright. The two not only corresponded with each other, they sent each other copies of their works. Nietzsche's theory of human existence as a series of struggles between stronger and weaker wills led Strindberg to conceive of the battle of the sexes primarily as psychological warfare between a superior male intellect and an inferior, but through cunning, an often victorious female intellect. For Nietzsche the will to life was the will to power through which each individual strives for self-realization or self-actualization. At one level a person is a multiplicity of instincts and drives, but all these are subsumed under the universal instinct for life which Nietzsche calls the will to power. In *The Gay Science* (1887) he wrote: "The struggle for survival is only an exception, a temporary restriction of the will to life; the great and small struggle revolves everywhere around preponderance, around growth and expansion, around power and in accordance with the will to power, which is simply the will to life." In fact he wrote to Strindberg after reading the latter's play *The Father* that he had been astonished to find "a work in which my own conception of love with war as its means and the deathly hate of the sexes as its fundamental law expressed in such a splendid fashion."

Strindberg's own experience of duality finds expression in Nietzsche's *The Birth of Tragedy* which discusses the opposing principles termed Apollonian and Dionysian. As one critic puts it: "The Apollonian has been taken to represent all aspirations in the direction of rationality, harmony, peace, contentment and quiet happiness. Apollonian is co-operative, uncompetitive, serene. In a word it holds that harmony should and can rule both in society and within the individual. But in man and therefore in nearly every society, there is also a Dionysian or passionate element. It promotes not only contest, rivalry, and strife, but also the intoxication of heroism, the ecstasy of pain and of self-destruction. It scorns mere happiness in favour of adventure, the sense of power, the exultation of struggle, even if it is a death struggle. . . . To seek difficulty, pain and madness is irrational, and therefore peculiarly human. . . . Moderation in all things is the fundamental doctrine of the Apollonian. Blake's 'The road of excess leads to the palace of wisdom' is its opposite."[2] These ideas, privileging the surrender to the irrational, echoed Strindberg's own, and he expressed his views in characteristically violent sexual imagery: "My spirit has received in its uterus a tremendous outpouring of seed from Friedrich Nietzsche, so that I feel as full as a pregnant bitch."

Strindberg wanted to see women as subordinate to men in nature's gendered hierarchy. He passionately believed that many of the problems of society were caused by those who attempted to challenge fate—as gender was dictated by birth so was social status. His failing marriage to Siri and his discovery of Nietzsche's Superman theories encouraged his views, yet all his wives were the career women he hated. Strindberg was also a friend of Munch, an expressionist painter whose series of paintings called "The Kiss" depicted women as vampires, sucking the blood and creativity out of men. This led him to boast: "I was always able to preserve my great brain from the influence of my sexual instinct so that I loved, coupled passionately and thought lucidly all the time, and then I wrote" (http://media.ucsc.edu/classes/thompson/strindberg/html)

Strindberg's misogyny manifested quite early in his career in *The Red Room* (1879). The Red Room was the meeting place in a small café in Stockholm of a society of needy journalists and artists whose failure and despair are set off against the prosperity of a typical bourgeois couple. In these stories, the disasters of the principal figures are shown as being precipitated by the selfishness and immorality of women.

Strindberg's marriage to Siri von Essen lasted from 1877 to 1891 and his second autobiographical novel, *A Madman's Defence* (1888), charts these turbulent years in a thinly disguised fictional form, calling himself Axel and Siri as Marie. It describes his courtship period, the baron's divorce, Axel's marriage after several backings-off; a series of ugly confrontations between Marie and Axel, followed by ecstatic reconciliations; his jealousy over her friendships with people in the theatre; his suspicions that, supported by a conspiracy of feminists and lesbians, she is trying to have him certified insane.

Yet there was a hairline division between his feelings of hatred and love. On the one hand, his attitude to women is that of a man overwhelmed with the physical, and when he is denouncing her as a creature who loves, beyond all things to deceive her husband, he expresses his abhorrence in the most violent terms: "If she can trick him into eating horseflesh without noticing it, she is happy." In the same year in which he wrote *Miss Julie*, he wrote to the poet Verner von Heidenstam "and if I had to define my present standpoint, it would be: Atheist, Christhater, Anarchist. . . . P.S. Woman, being small and foolish, and therefore evil, should be suppressed like barbarians and thieves. She is useful only as an ovary and womb." (See http://www.film education.org/secondary/Miss Julie/docs/strindberg.html)

Thus an important theme in all his plays is that of male-female conflict. These conflicts are really trials of strength, for Strindberg's men and women are locked in a Nietzschean battle of wills. The stronger character is the one who can more easily shake off the guilt in his past in order to attack with fewer encumbrances and reservations. Strindberg proclaimed the crippling consequences of guilt more than a decade before Sigmund Freud, although like Freud he met with bitter resistance and condemnation. The complications have to do not only with what the characters want but what they are. Almost all the conflicts are coloured by self-dissatisfaction; that is, they are seconded by internal conflicts in the characters themselves, who seem unsure about both what they want and what they are. (*European Writers*, Vol. 7, 1743)

Yet, as Gilman points out his anti-female biases were, as he himself put it 'the reverse side of my fearful attraction towards the other sex' and that he wrote to the critic Edvard Brandes that "my misogyny is only theoretical, and I can't live a day without supposing that I warm my soul at the flame of their unconscious, vegetable way of life." (87) Strindberg even defended himself from charges of misogyny: "I have said that woman is what she is, but I have always loved some woman and been a father. Whoever, therefore, calls me a woman-hater is a blockhead, a liar or a noodle. Or all three together." The foundations of the familiar Strindbergian encounter—a quasi-Darwinian struggle across sex and class lines, is thus clearly established. It is an inexorable struggle, capable of no solution and, given the tormented state of mind of the playwright himself, its expression can only be tragic.

References

1. Richard Gilman, *The Making of Modern Drama* (Yale, 1972; A Da Capo Paperback, rpt. 1972), p. 83.
2. Joseph Wood Krutch, "Modernism," *Modern Drama* (Ithaca: Cornell University Press, 1953), pp. 35-36.

Chapter VII

Miss Julie: Theme, Characterization and Style

Miss Julie is Strindberg's searing dramatization of the social reality of class structures, the physiological reality of gender patterns and the psychological reality of sexual conflict. It reflects Strindberg's own experience of the tensions of the man-woman relationship and his ambivalent feelings with regard to his parentage. It was one of the paradoxes of his life that while he identified himself with his mother's proletarian background, as is evident in the title of his autobiographical novel *The Son of a Servant*, he was also his father's son, proud and fastidious with aristocratic inclinations. The social Darwinism at the core of the play is apparent in Strindberg's assertion in his preface that "the alternation of rising and falling is one of life's principal charms" and that though the bird of prey devours the dove, "it happens just as often that the bee kills the lion or at least drives it mad."

Both Julie and Jean are caught up in the rigid codes dictated by their position in the social hierarchy. Both instinctively make the attempt to break away. Julie the aristocrat is seen as genetically corrupt, a victim of biologically decadent ideas about female emancipation, disturbing the natural patterns in its refusal to accept its biological role as wife and mother. Strindberg's hatred of the "new woman" or the "third sex" as he called them and whom he detested for their masculinity, infidelity, competitiveness and unmaternal attitudes, is evinced in the harsh delineation of Julie's character in the preface. He describes her as a "modern character," a "half-woman, the man-hater," "a type who thrusts herself forward, selling herself nowadays for power, decorations, distinctions, diplomas, as formerly for money. The type implies degeneration. . . . But fortunately they perish, either because they cannot come to terms with reality, or because their repressed instincts break out uncontrollably, or again because their hopes of catching up with men are shattered."

Given Strindberg's interest in psychology, his characterization of Julie is that of a hysteric. The word 'hysteria' is derived from the Greek word 'hustera', meaning 'womb'. In ancient times, people believed in demon possession of the female reproductive system. In Strindberg's day, hysteria increasingly came to refer not only to theories of innate degeneracy, but to sexual disturbances. Specifically, it was thought that women became hysterics when they failed or refused to accept their sexual desires. (www.sparknotes.com/drama/missjulie)

Julie has been brought up by an aggressively emancipated mother and raised to mistrust and hate men and compete with them at riding, hunting and even farming. Like her mother, who had a lover and hoped to dominate her father, she wishes to enslave and dominate men. When the father rebelled and reestablished control over his household, the mother burnt down the house and put him in a situation where, as Julie tells Jean, "he couldn't bring an action, couldn't pay his wife's lover, nor prove it was his wife's money." It was her mother's way of revenging herself on the man who had made himself master in his own house.

Julie is a divided soul, caught between allegiance to her mother (woman) and love-hate towards her father (man) for his role in allowing her to be brought up "to despise [her] sex, to be half-woman, half-man." She has inherited the primitive, intense passions of her mother and the neurotic aristocratic tendencies of her father. Julie's 'taming' of her fiancé by making him jump over her riding crop becomes an instance of her desire for power, an activity involving sexual humiliation. The breaking of the crop, with its phallic connotations, symbolizes the destruction of a power that has falsely appropriated male domain. In fact, Julie's giving herself to her father's servant is seen as an act of defiance and revenge against him, a self-destructive means of avenging her mother's submission to the male patriarchal order which has regained control over the family.

Strindberg's obvious sympathies for the father-figure makes him view the mother (and by default, Julie) as another of the devious women whose aim is to challenge the natural authority of the male, and who often gain their victories through cunning. She is in the same class as Laura in *The Father*—the aggressive, deceitful, manipulative wife. As he wrote: "Woman already by nature is instinctively villainous." For him, the ideal woman was represented by the good wife-mother. The opposite, the New Woman, threatened the existing image of the Ideal and was seen as vampire or whore. He believed that the attempts of women to obtain social equality were challenges to the natural law. The sexual rebellion instilled in Julie by her mother clashes with the traditional social conditioning of women.

Freud made the assumption that the mechanism of the mind is charged with only one type of energy which is basically sexual. Deflecting this instinct by means of reason creates a state of torment which Freud called neurotic. Julie is thus a split personality with male aggression and female submission co-existing uneasily within her. In the beginning, she assumes the active role of a man, deliberately crossing the boundaries of class and sex by dancing with the gamekeeper and asking Jean, the valet, to dance with her. Her position gives her power and she uses it shamelessly, behaving in a coquettish manner flipping him in the face with her handkerchief, forcing him to discard his livery, drinking beer with him, insisting that he kiss her hand, and even her shoe. Her hatred and disgust for men is only the reverse side of her irresistible fascination for them. It is her aggression that initiates the seduction and she is primarily responsible for the sexual abandon that breaks down the gap between mistress and servant and thereby destroys both her social identity and her psychological equilibrium. Strindberg believed that women survive in the sex duel because the chivalric code protects them. Once Julie has sacrificed this protection by consorting with a man of low birth, she is left vulnerable. At this level, the retribution that falls on her is seen as deserved. She becomes the feminine "other," bent on conquering men and ultimately destroying them, and therefore one that has to be repressed and controlled in order to maintain social order.

Societal class is a major theme in the play and Julie is caught between staying within her class and breaking from it. Her inner struggle is seen through the symbolism of her recurring dream of degradation and fall and she makes an existentialist choice to act out her perverse desires. Dreams are an ambiguous reflection of the repressed desire. Thus Julie's dream of being on top of a pillar and wanting to fall, not having the courage to jump, yet wanting to go "right down on the ground" is an acknowledgement of her unconscious urge to degrade herself, show weakness as a woman and fulfil her biological purpose, thus turning herself away from her unnatural upbringing: "something in me cried out for your seed," she says.

Strindberg's overtly naturalistic intention of showing the effects of heredity and environment on personality is undercut by a psychological probing into the hidden motivations of human behaviour. This makes him sympathize with her tragic fate; to a considerable extent he identifies with Julie, the child fatally divided by the divisions between her parents. As she rushes headlong into ruin, Strindberg manages to evoke in us compassion for what he calls "her desperate fight against nature." He sees in it a "Romantic inheritance," a desire for "happiness." Strindberg knew intimately the profound conflict between the male and female sides of his own nature and this is what he transposes into his characterization of Julie.

This conflict has been analyzed by Julia Kristeva in *Revolution in Poetic Language,* where she points out that if a woman identifies with the mother, she ensures her exclusion from and marginality in relation to the patriarchal order. Mother-identification results in a failure to enter the symbolic order, a path that ends in psychosis or suicide. It makes for powerlessness. If however, she identifies with the father—makes herself in his image (in Julie's case, her desire for authority and power) then she ends up supporting the same patriarchal order that excludes and marginalizes her as a woman. (See Su-lin Yu: "Reconstructing Western Female Subjectivity" in http://social.chass.ncsu.edu/jourvert/v7is1/slyu.htm.) Julie verbalizes this tension when she says: "For that matter everything is strange. Life, human beings, everything, just scum drifting about on the water until it sinks—down and down."

In the first place her liaison with Jean is seen not only as an arrogant assertion of power over men, but an act of rebellion against the norms of a patriarchal society. It is the attempt of the repressed female sensibility to triumph over the impersonal male order. It is significant that the seduction begins after the departure of her father, and reaches a conclusion with his return. But for all her arrogance and condescension, her innate naivete about the world outside the boundaries of her social station, spells danger. She imagines that she is "doing the people an honour by attending the ball when I'm mistress of the house," even as the people "stand grinning at her too from behind the doors." She tells Jean, "I know our people and I love them, just as they do me," even as the peasants sing a bawdy song mocking her. And most importantly, though she tries to gently close the social gap, "tonight we're all just people enjoying a party. There's no question of class," she cannot understand that in giving in to her blandishments, Jean is merely attempting to climb the social ladder without any commitment to love. It is here that the play dramatizes the ambiguity that shows up in the preface. Far from being a monstrous aberration of nature, Julie is seen as victim of the fatality of circumstance. Her struggle to break free of her psychological prison is a futile one, and liberation can come only in death.

Strindberg wrote about sex with absolute realism, dramatizing the compound of love, hate, fury and desire that characterizes relationships. In *Miss Julie*, once the sexual encounter is complete, there is a complete reversal of roles. Now she becomes the weaker entity and Jean uses his sexual superiority to brutalize her and to combat her superiority to him in terms of class. He now treats her as an equal, fit to be insulted and despised. As all her romantic illusions of eternal love are crushed one by one, she is paralyzed. Having lost her power, she is rendered helpless, unable to think for herself, totally without will. She has to be commanded like a servant.

Julie's yearning for lilacs and the sunrise, her fantasies about Lake Como "where the sun always shines and at Christmas time there are green trees and glowing oranges" is seen both as life-furthering affirmation and as illusory. It is an escape fantasy which confirms that there is no escape. It serves the paradoxical function of adding poignancy to the situation even as it emphasizes its finality. The frenzy of desperation that makes her even agree to live life on Jean's terms—("I shall sit in the office. . . . I'd make out the bills. There's a life for you") progressively heightens the tragic pathos of a woman who "yearned for wings" and is tied down by the conflicting drives and desires of the self.

The killing of the bird is symbolic of the duality that encompasses Julie's character. On the one hand, it is seen as a symbolic castration of a woman already established as inappropriately masculine. On the other hand, she, like the bird, is the symbolic victim of a cruel execution. The decapitating of the greenfinch ("The only living thing that cares for me," says Julie) acts as a catalyst in her relationship with Jean, goading her into expressing a brutal death wish for the entire male sex. It is accompanied by a wish for an end to her own life, death being seen as a victory despite her sexual defeat: "Oh how wonderful to make an end of it all—a real end! He has a stroke and dies and that's the end of all of us. Just peace and quietness . . . eternal rest. The coat of arms broken on the coffin and the Count's line extinct" while the valet's line will continue in the orphanage, the gutter and the jail. The sanctity of the class divisions that Julie had been impelled to violate is thus restored.

The play, however, mirrors Julie's "vacillating" self and her character fluctuates from moment to moment. In her state of frenzied confusion, Julie flings herself into the arms of Kristin for protection and help. But Strindberg, despite his misogyny, had an uncommon insight into the hypocrisy of his society's gender expectations and morality. He reserves some of his harshest criticism for Kristin "a female slave, full of servility and sluggishness acquired in front of the kitchen fire, and stuffed full of morality and religion which are her cloak and scapegoat. She goes to church as a quick and easy way of unloading her household thefts (we have been told that she has been taking a commission for the groceries and bribes from the butcher) on to Jesus." Kristin believes in the social chain of command as firmly as she embraces the hierarchical piety of the church. But though she pays glib lip-service to the teachings of the Bible, there is neither compassion nor kindness in her. As a parting shot she even makes sure that all avenues of escape for Julie are cut off. Her uncomplicated and uncompromising attitudes throw into sharp relief the tormented conflicts within Julie

Rejected by Kristin's holier-than-thou morality and smug pietism, Julie's dejection and despair reaches its lowest point. Her speech, painting before Kristin a rosy picture of their life together ("Wouldn't that be splendid?," "You've no idea how nice it is," "just like in fairy tales," "You'll sit like a queen in the kitchen.") begins *presto tempo*, but winds down to a dull, exhausted weariness as reality overpowers the desperate fantasy ("of course it rains there a little now and then—but—(dully)—the sun must shine there too sometimes—even though it seems gloomy"). In the midst of Kristin's homilies about faith, sin, forgiveness and grace, one line alone registers in Julie's shattered mind—"with Him the last shall be the first." Her comment "then I suppose He does respect the last," points to the complete reversal that has taken place. She is now no longer the aristocratic master, but as low as the reviled servant, and the respect that was concomitant with her status has passed away.

It is at this point that another reversal takes place. Given to disgrace and even to death, Julie's character is transformed even as it disintegrates. Abandoned both by Jean and Kristin, Julie turns to her own self and in refusing to put the blame elsewhere and taking it on herself, she regains her position as morally superior. Strindberg lauds this "fatal preoccupation with honour" in the preface. He writes: "Even if the father had felt impelled to take no vengeance, the daughter would have taken vengeance on herself, as she does here, from that innate or acquired sense of honour which the upper-classes inherit. . . . It is a very beautiful thing . . . the nobleman's hara-kiri, the Japanese law of inner conscience." It is a rising again after the fall. Unlike Kristin, she refuses to "push the responsibility on to Jesus. . . . No, I'm too proud and—thanks to my father's teaching—too intelligent." Her willingness to die to atone for the sacrifice of her honour endorses the aristocratic principle that the servant can never reach. "I must take the blame and bear the consequences," she tells Jean. Sympathetic identification is firmly established when she touches the area of heroic self-assertion. As she walks from the kitchen to the barn with the razor in her hand, she walks towards death. She is the refined aristocrat succumbing in the struggle with the coarsely proletarian Jean, the "race-builder," the progenitor of a new social species. Strindberg very clearly sees her as representative of a dying order and laments that the pygmies will inherit the earth.

Her suicide can, in one way, be seen as an act of atonement for her rebellion against the social norms. She has realized that the barriers of rank reared through the ages by wealth and power, is not flung aside with impunity. It can also be seen as a resolution to the self-divisions that have tormented her. Julie's death by suicide was suggested to Strindberg by the death of the Swedish writer Victoria Benedictsson, who had hoped to form an alliance literary and sexual, with the famous critic Georg Brandes. Despondent and disillusioned, feeling neither respected nor loved, she made several suicide attempts, ultimately slashing her throat with a razor. Strindberg started writing his play shortly after this incident; and he follows the account of Victoria's childhood in Julie's blaming her neurotic disposition and her perverse and self-destructive sexual desires on her upbringing.

While on the one hand, the suicide signifies her victory over circumstance, it may, on the other hand, signify her defeat by the patriarchal order where the Count's authority demands her death and the razor which is to be the instrument of her death is put into her hands by another avenging male, Jean. Her power games become self-defeating as she fails in her attempts to change her destiny. The "multiplicity of motives" that Strindberg aimed at is very much in evidence.

Paradox also governs Strindberg's portrayal of Jean, the valet. As he describes his "dual, indeterminate" character in the preface, it is a "blend" of admiration and clear-eyed criticism. He is a labourer's son who had educated himself towards becoming a gentleman; he has learnt easily, has well-developed senses, a sense of beauty; he is an "aristocrat" who has learned the mannerisms of good society and is, therefore, rising. Sexually he is the aristocrat because of his virility, his keener senses ("Have you ever noticed how smooth oats are? Soft to touch as human skin") and his capacity for taking the initiative. He has the upper hand over Miss Julie because he is a man. He is a "race-builder" with aspirations of becoming a Romanian count

On the other hand, he is thick-skinned enough not to have scruples; he is polished, but vulgar within; he dresses tastefully, but there is no guarantee of his personal cleanliness. He is callous and calculating, "having both the slave's brutality and the master's lack of squeamishness." When he speaks the truth, which is not often, he says what is favourable to himself rather than what is true. Strindberg continues: "The slave mentality expresses itself in his worship of the Count (the boots) and his religious superstitions; but he worships the Count chiefly because he holds that higher position for which Jean himself is striving. And this worship remains even when he has won the daughter of the house and seen how empty is that lovely shell." His lack of sensitivity ensures that he "emerges from the battle unscathed and probably, ends his days as a hotelkeeper."

On the one hand, therefore, the play presents Jean as the predestined master. With his virility and strength, he is the epitome of the masculine principle. His sexual appeal is unmistakable. Julie calls him a "big, strong man. . . . What muscles!" He exudes a powerful sense of purpose in his desire to get on in the world and his dream of lying under a tree in a thick and dark wood and then of climbing the tree into bright sunlight and robbing a bird's nest of its golden eggs is a dream of aspiration. He rouses sympathy as representing an oppressed and deprived section of society. He tells Julie: "I lived in a labourer's hovel with seven other children and a pig, out in the grey fields where there isn't a single tree." Images of squalor abound in the characterization of Jean. He is associated with the kitchen garden, the onion bed, the stinking sewer through which he is forced to make his exit, the weed pile with its prickly thistles and damp, rank earth, in contrast to the rose-garden and the honey-suckle covered pavilion of Julie's world. The Count's park with its apple trees is, to him, the Garden of Eden and Julie walking among the roses in her pink dress and white stockings, becomes "a symbol of the hopelessness of ever getting out of the class [he] was born in."

But Jean confines his aspirations and romanticism to changes in economic and social status. And the sympathy built up for him is undercut by his coarseness, cruelty and commonness, which makes him value wine because it is expensive, indulge in petty thieving, and butcher the bird without compunction. He wants aristocrats to be above him and yet wants to despise them. Familiarity with them breeds contempt. "Perhaps," he says, "there isn't as much difference between people as one's led to believe."

Once the sexual encounter is complete, the distinction of class is rendered meaningless. Jean ruthlessly flaunts his male superiority before Julie. He takes full advantage of his power over her to brutalize her emotionally, cruelly pointing out that without money, she is of no value to him, callously wiping out all ideas of love and romance by making it clear that for him, it was no more than an encounter on the way to more serious matters. "We make love for fun in our spare time, but we haven't all day and all night for it like you." It is his way of punishing her for destroying the image of the woman he might aspire to serve. Jean takes great pains to emphasize her degradation, linking her with a rotten branch and equating her behaviour with that of animals and prostitutes. He even throws her a coin to clear off his debt towards the woman he has ruined. He answers Julie's bitter recriminations with cutting sarcasm: "I can't deny there's a certain satisfaction in finding that what dazzled one below was just moonshine, . . . that there's powder on that lovely cheek, that polished nails have black tips. That the handkerchief is dirty although it smells of scent. . . . It hurts to see you fallen so low you're far lower than your own cook. Hurts like when you see the last flowers of summer lashed to pieces by rain and turned to mud."

Their fateful relationship takes them in precisely opposite directions. As Brustein points out: "Julie's descent, therefore, is a movement from spirit to flesh, motivated by her attraction to dirt and death. She unconsciously desires to degrade herself, to be soiled and trampled on, and when she falls she ruins her entire house. . . . By contrast, Jeans's ascent is associated with cleanliness and life, and is a movement from the flesh to the spirit. Like Julie he is trying to escape the conditioning of his childhood—a childhood in which filth, muck and excrement played a large part. . . . For just as Julie is attracted to his class, so he is impelled towards hers." (336-37)

As a naturalistic drama, *Miss Julie* focuses on the struggle of the two main characters for power, dictated by the forces of heredity and environment. It is both a sexual and class struggle. Ostensibly, Jean as the stronger male figure, the one with the skills and the ambition to succeed, is the one who is the fittest to survive and this is in consonance with Strindberg's idea, expressed in the preface, of the desirability of the "national parks [being] cleared of ancient rotting trees which have stood too long in the way of others equally entitled to a period of growth." Seen in this light, Miss Julie depicts the destruction of a decadent member of the aristocracy by a rising member of the lower classes. Strindberg's notorious hostility towards women who challenged male dominance in any form or tried to usurp it finds vindication in the manner in which Julie's confusion with regard to her sexual identity leads to her ruin.

On the other hand, this was the time when Strindberg responded to Nietzsche's theories championing the "great" against the "small." From this viewpoint, the victory goes to Julie, for the ending re-inforces our sense of Jean's slave mentality. Julie makes the existentialist choice that liberates her. Though she loses all volition and enters a trance-like state in which she has to be commanded to act, her decision not to live devoid of honour is tragically heroic. Conversely, Jean reverts to his status of a menial, quaking at the sound of the Count's voice.

The ending is open enough to lend itself to several interpretations—one of them being that after the innumerable power reversals, both Julie and Jean are reduced to a joint submission to the Count, who is master and father. Julie has authority over Jean partly because she is her father's daughter and Jean has authority over her because he has the Count's power as a man. The Count's authority demands Jean's return to servitude and Julie's death. As Strindberg himself notes, he has kept "the unhappy spirit of the father above and behind the action."

It could also be said that at this point, Julie identifies herself with her mother: "my mother is revenged again, through me." The unconscious mind is shown to impinge on the conscious as Julie enters a trance-like, hypnotic state in which she sees, as in a hallucination: "the whole room turned to smoke—and you look like a stove—a stove like a man in black with a tall hat—your eyes are glowing like coals when the fire is low—and your face is a white patch like ashes." Patrick Roberts comments: "In this superb image of destructive sexuality father and lover coalesce as a single avenging persecutory figure. The figure also beckons her to peace—the peace of death, suggesting the seemingly reparatory aspect of suicide, and thus the magnitude of the preceding guilt."[1] The ambivalence is of a piece with the fact that Strindberg's naturalistic tenets were also undercut by his interest in what he called a "soul-complex," the "multiplicity of motives" that goes beyond those directed by heredity and environment. His conscious intentions become subject to the pressures of imaginative creativity in the process of writing. It is at such points that naturalism blends into expressionism. The almost coma-like state to which fatigue, inner tension, dishonour, and the aphrodisiacal atmosphere of the evening has reduced, Julie also has the effect of hypnotizing the audience into a dreamlike awareness of the dramatic proceedings. The spectators become as blurred and vague in their perception as Julie and are compelled toward the final resolution as inexorably as she is.

In his essay "On Modern Drama and Modern Theatre" published in 1889, Strindberg noted that the "new" naturalist drama pays more attention to character description than to plot, that the unities of time and place are observed and that, in "searching for the significant motif," the playwrights focus on "life's two poles, life and death . . . the fight for the spouse, for the means of subsistence, for honour—all these struggles—with their battle cries of woe . . . during which one head a new philosophy of life, conceived as a struggle." It was also in this essay that he put down his famous dictum "by means of a table and two chairs . . . [to] present the most powerful conflicts of life" and this by resorting to "the discoveries of modern psychology."[2] Thus, the one-act play allowed Strindberg to present the existential or metaphysical conflict between characters as well as with some force outside them which they cannot master. Every unessential or distracting element is removed so as to focus relentlessly on the fundamental opposition that is being enacted. As he writes in the preface: "I have come to the conclusion that our capacity for illusion is disturbed by the intervals, during which the audience has time to reflect and escape from the suggestive influence of the author-hypnotist." Hence his emphasis is on maintaining the "illusion."

To keep the plot simple and intense, Strindberg had to find a substitute for the complications that furnished action and suspense in conventional drama. He found this in a system of symbols and parallelisms, that become the means of presenting the unconscious drives and desires of his characters dramatically and of creating density of meaning without being obtrusive. The setting of this play which deals with rebellion against the constraints of rank and morality is aptly Midsummer's Eve, a festival of pagan and sexual origins, an occasion for crossing the boundaries of social order. The lines demarcating class are clearly drawn out in the two spaces that frame the action, the kitchen which is home to the servants like Kristin the cook and Jean the valet, and the courtyard leading to the rest of the house, with its fountain, with a cupid, lilac bushes in flower and the tops of Lombardy poplars, all indicative of an upper-class life style. Connecting the two are the bell and the speaking tube through which the absent count gives his orders and the pair of large riding boots with spurs which are an image of his authority. The conspicuous placing of these boots symbolize the all-encompassing power of the father-figure, and it is significant that Jean, in an attempt to deflect Julie's dangerously blatant flirtation, takes up the boots to signal his position as a menial. The play comes full circle with Jean, after having experienced temporary power with his sexual conquest of Julie, is once again reduced to a cringing lackey at the ringing of the bell which announces the count's orders for his boots and coffee. Jean's livery is a sign of his status as servant, and it is significant that Julie begins her seduction by insisting that he take it off and wear his black coat instead: "You look quite the gentleman in that get-up. Charming," she tells him. As Strindberg points out in the Preface: "His inferiority is mainly due to the social environment in which he lives and he can probably shed it with his valet's livery."

Julie's pets become mirror images for her own situation. Her dog, ironically named Diana, after the virgin goddess, in its coupling with a mongrel, is acting in the same way as its mistress in her relationship with a servant; while the caged bird that Julie wants to take with her becomes symbolic of the imprisonment of her romantic spirit within a body torn with conflicting sexual desires. The decapitation of the bird on the chopping block is an assertion on Jean's part of brutal male power, with Julie as the symbolic victim. On the other hand, the reference to the beheading of John the Baptist, makes Julie another Salome bent on destruction of the male and using the same kind of cunning to gain a devious sexual victory.

Strindberg adds depth and resonance to his characterization through the use of biblical allusions which throw a symbolic aura over his naturalistic play. Julie calls Jean a Joseph, referring to the story in Genesis of the seduction of Joseph by the wife of Potiphar, an officer of Pharaoh's guard. Her fictitious charge of sexual assault reinforces the idea of woman as a scheming enemy of man, bent on ruining him, an idea that is clearly evident in Strindberg's presentation of Julie. Unlike the biblical Joseph, who was sold into servitude, however, Jean is neither "discreet" nor "wise" and his fate is not to be clothed in "vestures of fine linen" and "a gold chain about his neck," like Joseph, but to shrink in servile fear at the Count's commands. Thus one rising is contrasted with another.

In another allusion, Jean's yearning for a paradisal state of happiness is mirrored through the Garden of Eden and the Tree of Life symbolism, of which, given his acquisitive nature, he is a despoiler. Linked to this, is the idea of the Fall, which has its own symbolic relevance in the play, and of Julie as Eve, the archetypal temptress, seducing man to taste forbidden fruit and thereby ruining him.

Ideas of salvation and redemption are brought to the forefront in the allusion to the two thieves who were crucified with Christ and one of whom was saved, as also in the reference to the Book of Revelation, where the great voice pronounces "I am Alpha and Omega, the first and the last. I am he that liveth and behold, I am alive for evermore." Julie comes to realize that her morality in accepting the blame and taking the consequences is truer than Kristin's distorted religiosity with its narrow-minded interpretations of Biblical teachings. On the one hand, she speaks of faith, grace and penitence; on the other she is piously vindictive: "and it is easier for a camel to go through the eye of a needle than for a rich man to enter into the Kingdom of God."

Strindberg charts the two extremes of class structure through the symbols of the rose garden and lilac flowers on the one hand and the onion bed with its weeds and thistles and damp rank earth on the other, the Turkish pavilion covered with honey-suckle and jasmine contrasted with the stinking sewer through which Jean is forced to make his exit. Images of filth point to the degradation of the lower class, but as Julie crosses the boundaries of class, she is mired in the same filth: "Oh God in heaven, put an end to my miserable life! Lift me out of this filth in which I'm sinking."

The element of fantasy in the play shows Julie reaching out for an ideal world in subconscious reaction to the sordid world that she inhabits. Her dreams of Lake Como "where the sun's always shining and the oranges shine in the trees and the laurels have fresh green leaves at Christmas time" and her memories of other Midsummer Days—"the leafy church—birch and lilac—the gaily spread dinner table, relatives, friends—evening in the park—dancing and music and flowers and fun," as well as memories of a world of refinement and beauty—her travels, the zoo in Hamburg, the theatre and the opera, the paintings of Rubens and Raphael, fairy-tale castles and the snow-covered Alps which she describes to an uncomprehending Kristin, all combine to heighten the pathos of Julie's situation. She is seen as a romantic soul "yearning for wings," crushed like "the last flowers of summer" and "turned to mud" The play dramatizes Strindberg's understanding of the tragic nature of man's irreconcilable impulses, whose nature he divined by an introspective understanding of the conflicts in his own experience, with its contradictions and ambivalences.

References

1. Patrick Roberts, "Strindberg: the Long and Cruel Struggle" in *The Psychology of Tragic Drama* (London: Routledge and Kegan Paul, 1975), pp. 63-66.

2. Egil Tornqvist, "The Strindbergian One Act Play," *Scandinavian Studies*, 68: 3 (1996), pp. 356-69.

Appendix

Strindberg's *The Father*

Any discussion of Strindberg's naturalistic period to which *Miss Julie* belongs must begin with *The Father*, where the statement made by one of the protagonists "Life between the sexes is strife" becomes the central idea of all the plays he wrote about this time. It is a drama about marriage, and many of Strindberg's personal experiences were involved in this highly emotional study of a struggle for power as a ruthless, aggressive woman tries to usurp the supposedly male prerogative of decision making. It reveals the full range of Strindberg's expectations and disappointments in woman as wife, daughter and mother. It is a savage collision of two wills, each seeking absolute mastery, and depicts the cunningly planned, systematic destruction of the husband by his wife.

The play was written at a point of time when Strindberg's marriage with Siri von Essen was near collapse and he was experiencing doubts as to the paternity of his first child, born two months after their wedding. He would make long unexplained journeys to find evidence of her guilt and then would come back and fall at her feet to beg forgiveness. He also suspected that his arch-rival Ibsen had used him as a model for the pathetic, cuckolded husband Hjalmar Ekdal in the play *The Wild Duck*. Another incentive to write on such a subject, as noted by Martin Lamm in his book on Strindberg, may have been an article by French sociologist Paul Lafargue about Euripides's play *The Oresteia*, which interpreted the classical Greek work as a dramatization of the birth of matriarchy and saw a similar struggle emerging in contemporary society. Matriarchy was not a benevolent concept to Strindberg, for to him it meant a world ruled by women who had abandoned their function as caring maternal beings in order to exercise power through the use of their irrational and possessive psyches. How this might be done and what the result could be is what Strindberg describes in *The Father.*[1]

The play is a dramatization of the conflicts that were surging within him—woman's ruthlessness in the struggle between man and wife, jealousy and paternity and the nagging fear that he was losing his mind. Peter Watts in the introduction to his translation of *The Father* notes two other obsessions during this period—the first was with Feminism, which infuriated him and led him to the idea of women as the greatest enemy.[2] The other was with the power of suggestion. He had been much impressed by Shakespeare's Othello and he was convinced that suggestion was a more subtle method of murder than poison or the knife. *The Father* depicts a battle between the Captain and his wife Laura over the future of their child. Their disagreement is over whether their daughter Bertha, aged seventeen, shall stay at home and become an artist, as Laura wishes, or go away and train to become a teacher, as the Captain wishes. Determined to have her way, Laura devises ways of undermining her husband's confidence. One of her most insidious weapons is the doubt that she allows to fester in his mind that he is not the father of Bertha. Her method is psychological torture

Initially, the Captain is seen as an inflexible, principled man, who though he presides over a house full of women, which he compares to a cage full of tigers, still manages to hold the upper hand: "I'll have no one, woman or child—encroaching on my rights." He manages to act as the patriarchal figure in every sphere: to manage his scholarly pursuits in his own way, to manage their property and to manage their child. He has done everything to assert himself, to become admirable and masterful and therefore, he feels, lovable, but he has not succeeded.

The harsh reality is that Laura is the stronger of the two and even the Captain recognizes her power: "Yes, when it comes to getting your own way you have the power of the devil," he says, though Laura herself is not fully conscious of how this is so: "It's odd, but I've never been able to look at a man without feeling I'm his superior." The Pastor, too, feels her innate strength: "How strong you are Laura, incredibly strong! You're like a fox in a trap, you'd rather bite off your own leg than let yourself be caught." In contrast the Captain, who knows that he has been an unwanted child and hence "born without a will" finds himself as weak as a child in front of this "superior, gifted being" he has married, tormented both by fascination and repulsion. As Laura mockingly tells him: "Your great strong body had no fibre, you were like an overgrown child."

It is very soon clear that Laura has a very different agenda in their marriage. Her goal is to have the Captain certified insane so that he loses legal claim to his daughter, because, according to her "a mother's nearer to the child." He has fulfilled his role as father and breadwinner and now there is no further need of him. She puts forward the suggestion that only she, not he, can really know whether Bertha is his natural child. As his suspicions mount, he sees himself as Hercules deprived of his club, very clearly a castration symbol, and Laura as Omphale "Rude strength brought down by scheming weakness." Images of destruction accumulate as the Captain describes himself as a half of a tree which has been cut apart and which is withering and dying, as Saturn who ate his own children. On the one hand he curses all women—mother, sister, lover, daughter, wife—as natural enemies. On the other is a strange eroticism that merges mother and mistress: "Lean over me, so that I can feel your breast. Oh, it's good to sleep on a woman's breast—a mother's or a mistress's, but a mother's is best." There is thus alternating tenderness and hostility, but as the mists of insanity cloud his brain, he utters a lament for the unrelenting pull of fate: "there are only shadows . . . my thoughts melt into thin air, and my brain grinds away at nothing, till it catches fire."

The play, says Gilman, is a "modern legend of ancient despair" and that it is informed "by something close to an ancient spirit of blood-feud." (93) Brustein, too, sees the two protagonists as figures of Aeschylean tragedy, "for like Agamemnon and Clytemnestra, the Captain and Laura are monolithic figures hewn out of granite and stripped of all character details extraneous to their warring natures." (328) There is something almost unconscious about the evil in Laura, an essential power that is uniquely and naturally Female; she achieves her ends as if impelled by instinct. In the harrowing final scene, the Captain who has been lured into a straitjacket, the terrifying symbol of the mental asylum, lies helpless at the nurse's breast, repudiating his child, then succumbing to a fatal stroke; Laura, embracing Bertha, cries, "My child! My own child!"

Nietzsche summed up the play when he wrote that he had been "astonished" to find "a work in which my own conception of love—with war as its means and the deathly hate the sexes as its fundamental law . . . is expressed in such a splendid fashion." (Gilman, 95) The first production created a storm, with critics trashing the unrelenting despair of Strindberg's vision and calling it "a bitter, unpoetic fruit on the arid tree of realism" (Marker, 109). Yet none could deny the author's "violent force" as Ibsen himself termed it, whereby he makes his characters wounded souls, uncertain and self-divided, relentlessly engaged in a bitter, destructive "battle of brains."

References

1. See *Major 20th Century Writers* (2nd ed., Vol. 5, Gale, Detroit and London, 1998, p. 2709.

2. *Three Plays by August Strindberg*, trans. Peter Watts (Penguin, 1958).

Destructive Personal Relationships in Strindberg's Plays

BRATI BISWAS
Dyal Singh (Eve.) College, University of Delhi

Reading through Strindberg's plays one finds, appearing as a recurring motif, the theme of man-woman relationship. As this is the primary relationship from which originate all other relationships, Strindberg's exploration of the tensions inherent in it, becomes his way of understanding the problems of the world. For Strindberg the world is divided between the Male and the Female principles. In *A Dream Play* (1901), he gives expression to his very unchristian conception of the world as being the product of a union between the Male and the Female principles, that of "Brahma, the divine primal force" and "Maya, the world mother"[1] as this union also represents for Strindberg the impossible coming together of two opposite forces, that of the spirit and the flesh, the world in consequence becomes, for Strindberg, the home of irreconcilable dualities, dualities which create the condition of perpetual strife in human lives. Thus, man, composed of these warring elements becomes a divided being, and this tension between his conflicting selves gets most evidently manifested in the battle of the sexes. Strindberg further uses the emblem of sexual conflict to represent social strife in his plays. The domestic sphere is a microcosm of the world and that which infects the most basic unit of society ultimately affects the whole society—the domestic thus translates into the universal.

Strindberg's life to a large extent explains his works and his philosophy. Taking a biographical approach, critics view Strindberg's fascination with the battle of the sexes as originating in his unhappy relationships with the women in his life and his divided sensibilities. Robert Brustein points to how Strindberg, the son of a servant and a *déclassé* aristocrat, regarded the circumstances of his birth as the source of all his later troubles. For instance he felt that, as a result of this union, his sympathies were continually divided between the peasant and the aristocrat, and his demeanour kept vacillating between peasant servility and aristocratic arrogance.[2]

His father had married his mother when she was pregnant with their fourth child, that is, Strindberg. Conceived out of wedlock and born prematurely, he felt he was unwanted and illegitimate. He described himself as a Pariah—outlawed from Paradise, a beggar, homeless among his own people. He lived a life of voluntary exile and imagined himself as a rebel—a kind of Faust figure. On the other hand he also felt that he was born without a 'Will' because he was born against his parent's will. This was essentially a passive and feminine self-image that was at odds with the rebel, masculine image. The dualism of his psyche gets reflected in his ambivalent feelings towards his mother and women in general. He adored his mother, and as he had to fiercely compete with his other eleven siblings for her attention he felt abandoned and rejected by his mother and hated her for preferring his other brothers to him. His Oedipal adoration of the mother made him harbour ambivalent feelings of hate, fear, and respect towards his father.

Strindberg was deeply attracted towards the figure of the chaste Madonna, a kind of older motherly woman who was sexless, kind and compassionate. Shortly before his death, in response to a questionnaire regarding which characteristic he prized most highly in a woman, he had replied 'Motherliness.' Helen Cooper notes, "like most men it was the Mary figure, the mother of Christ, he loved in women and the Eve figure he loathed. Eve, who wouldn't blindly submit to authority," a modern emancipated woman who was masculine, unfaithful, competitive, and unmaternal. Things get complicated when these two distinct categories of women merge to form the image of the Spiderwoman, a mother figure who is sexually desirable and who is obsessed with female domination. She is a kind of vampire that sucks away a man's virility and emasculates him. The wife as both mother and the mistress taints the relationship with the stain of incest. Laura in *The Father* represents such a type; she is a nurse, mother, wife and mistress all rolled into one. Laura cleverly manipulates these roles to effectively emasculate the Captain and reduce him to the level of a helpless child by the end of the play.

Strindberg was both attracted and repelled by women. He married beautiful, talented women who he believed also had a maternal side. He sought in his women an emblem of sensuous maternity—a combination of the Madonna and Eve, the chaste mother and the erotic belle. His first wife, Siri Von Essen, epitomized the ideal woman, fair haired and blue eyed with the face of a child. When Strindberg met her, she was already a wife and mother. He was captivated by her Madonna image and convinced himself that his love for her was purely spiritual. He married her in 1877, after her divorce from Baron Wrangel, a Guards Officer. His marriage to Siri, a moderately successful actress had its share of happy and turbulent moments. The marriage lasted nearly fourteen years and ended owing to Strindberg's growing jealousy and paranoia. On his deathbed he confessed that Siri was the only woman he had truly loved. His other two marriages to authoress Frida Uhl in 1893 and actress Harriet Bosse in 1901 too failed. Strindberg felt threatened by their success; he also suffered from persecution complex and feared that the feminists were plotting to kill him. The castrating, emasculating, vampirish women of his plays probably have their origins in this fear.

Thus his neurosis partly contributes to his ambivalent representation of the man-woman relationship.[3]

Nevertheless, as Strindberg was able to objectify his inner conflicts, and to the extent his characters reflect the universal predicaments of mankind, they and their motivations, cannot all be mere reflections of Strindberg's personality. Thus, though Strindberg's philosophy stems from, and expresses his psychological tensions, its ultimate significance lies in its universal appeal. The attempt of this paper is to focus, not on the artist's psychology only but also explore the dimensions of his philosophy as it become manifested in his work.

In my attempt to explore the causes, consequences and nature of the destructive personal relationships in Strindberg's plays, I will be focusing on the following plays, *The Father* (1887), *Miss Julie* (1888), *Creditors* (1890), *The Link* (1897) *A Dream Play* (1902) and *The Ghost Sonata* (I907). As *The Road to Damascus* (1898) is central to Strindberg's philosophy, on this theme, I also intend in my discussion of these plays, to briefly refer to this trilogy.

Hummel's statement in *The Ghost Sonata* (1907) that his "entire life's been like a book of stories . . . all different . . . [but] strung together on a sort of recurring theme"[5] illustrates the nature of Strindberg's plays, all of which are linked through the theme of destructive and stultifying relationships. In this chain, Strindberg's play *The Link* (1897), marks the end of his naturalistic phase and the beginning of his expressionistic phase.[6] The Naturalistic phase spans the years 1886-1889. The Inferno years intervening, *To Damascus* (1898) marks the beginning of the new phase. Coming midway between the two phases, it contains the essence of what he has already dealt with, in detail, and also suggests many of the ideas he was to develop in his Dream plays. Thus it would be convenient, for this once, to discard chronology and begin the discussion on the problem of destructive relationships with an analysis of this play of his middle period.

The Link presents in a compact form the nature of the conflict between the sexes. It begins with a consideration of the legal outcome of this conflict (i.e. divorce) and then uses it, to further reflect on the human problems behind it. The Sheriff, in the opening scene presents legalistically the complexity of the problem, "in this case [i.e. the man-woman relationship] it is not easy to tell who is guilty, for both parties are at once complainants and defendants" (I.i, p. 20). In other words each in himself is both the victim and the victimizer; victims of their own prejudices, they victimize themselves and others, by entering into false relationships.

The protagonists of this play, the Baron and the Baroness, are shown as isolated individuals; victims of their prejudices, they cannot come together at any point. At the onset of the play we see them idealistically agreeing to refrain from mutual recriminations, but as soon as the proceedings begin they immediately start to accuse each other (I.i & ix, pp. 22, 30). That they could ever have come together to create a relationship seems surprising. But one has only to take a close look at their habit of deliberately masking their selfish drives, through idealisms, to explain their coming together. We see that though the illusion of conformity created by their idealisms allowed them to come together, the resultant relationship is basically a false one and hence prone to disruptive forces from within and without. Thus, at the slightest instigation the masks are thrown off and the latent violence and aggression gets unleashed. For example, in the course of the play, the Baron's selfishness is slowly exposed. We see that, though the Baron had, sworn to have destroyed the documents establishing his wife's adultery, for the idealistic reason of love, he in fact had preserved them in order to take revenge, which he does by frustrating his wife's claim to the child and proving his power over her.

The falseness of the relationship further gives rise to ambivalences within it. When these ambivalences get further aligned to the basic opposition between the sexes they give rise to abnormal tendencies in love relationships. The Baron for instance suggests that the Baroness' love is masochistic, because she loved him most when he was unfaithful to her. (I.x, p. 37).[7] Calling her abnormal could be the Baron's way to taking revenge and justifying his infidelity. The Baroness on the other hand takes her revenge, by insidiously negating the Baron's maleness by bringing up his son as a girl. The Baron unconsciously alerts us to the fact when he states:

> Our son has your body, but my soul, and that soul you cannot rid him of. In him you will have me back when you least expect it; in him you will find my thoughts, my tastes, my passions, and for this reason you will hate him one day, as you hate me now. That is what I fear! (I.xiii, p. 42)

The Baron's fear of her hatred is legitimate, because we realise that by thwarting her son's growth into manhood, the Baroness is symbolically castrating her husband, and effectively taking away from him his hope of immortality through the child. In her attempts to undercut the male identity by feminizing it, she resembles a type of Omphale, who recurrently appears in Strindberg's plays and is viewed as a vampire.

In these relations between the sexes, love and hate coexist, and the resultant conflict creates the destructive spectacle of the "slaughter house." Hatred in fact "is the lining of the coat of love" (I.xi, p. 33). The play also suggests that there is no escape from this conflict and the situation of mutual lies and faithlessness it creates. Though the Baron and the Baroness contemplate both the options of separating or starting all over again, they are all the time acutely aware of the impossibility of doing so. Though they "have gone too far" and "are enemies of life" (I.x, p. 37) they cannot separate; the child ties them and in fact becomes the emblem of their imprisonment—in whom they "must ever meet without wishing to do so" (I.x, p. 38). They are curiously tied to each other, like the two sides of a personality. This is most clearly illustrated through the Baron's experience, "I have struck you down, and I am bleeding to death myself, for your blood is mine" (I.xiii, p. 41). It also suggests that the impulse to destroy the 'other' inevitably becomes self-destructive. And as such, the destruction of a relationship results in the destruction of both the partners.[9]

The Link also suggests that the characters are not solely to be blamed for their contradictions. Born with a sex, or into a class from which they cannot escape, they continually aspire towards the opposite. For example, the sorrow of the Baroness' life, like many other women in Strindberg's canon, is that she "was not born a man" (I.xii, p. 43) and therein lies her hatred of men and her desire to undermine them. Heredity too plays its part in creating these riven characters; driven by "evil tendencies, hatred and wild passions" from which there is no respite (I.xvi, p. 47). It represents a force beyond their control and introduces an element of fatality into the relationships.

This play's explanation of the universal nature of the conflicts anticipates the philosophy of the dream plays. "As everything . . . on this earth is imperfect" and "human nature is full of falsehood and dissimulation," a state of continual strife and pain becomes the essence of human life.

The Father (1887) portrays the tragedy of Man tainted with inherent antagonisms and dualities.[10] This is because "Men and women seek to destroy each other in the act of loving and creating new life, and the new life is itself always guilty . . . by the relationships, it is inevitably born into. For it is used as weapon and prize in the parent's continuing struggle, and is itself unwanted . . . [and thus is] haunted by the desires of an impossible return"[11] And the cycle goes on, perpetuating itself through each generation.

The Captain in *The Father* is the product of such a union. Insecure and suffering from the sense of an incomplete self, his tragedy lies in his attempts to complete himself through a woman and the fatal ambivalences it generates.[12] As he himself states, "my father and mother did not want me and consequently I was born without a will. I naturally enough thought that I was completing myself when you and I became one, and therefore you got the upper hand" (II.v, pp. 84-85). But Laura's earlier statement that she first entered his life as his "second mother" (83) reflects the ambivalence of his feelings and his actions. By seeking in his wife both a sexual partner and a mother surrogate, he inevitably riddled her with his ambivalences and dualities, thus creating a situation which is best expressed through Laura's words:

> Yes, so it was, and therefore I loved you as my child. But you know, you must have seen, when the nature of your feelings changed and you appeared as my lover, I blushed and the joy of your embraces turned to remorse as if my blood were ashamed. The mother became the mistress. Ugh! (II.v, p. 84)

Yet, in it she also suggests her own ambivalences, that as a woman, she "could love a man truly only as a mother" and thus the sexual relationship involves for her "the shame of incest."[13] Inherent in her dualities is the suggestion that they have been created not only by the Captain's conflicting demands on her, but also by forces that are beyond her control.

This fact becomes clear in Laura's explanation of the Captain's mistake:

> There was your mistake. The mother was your friend, you see, but the woman was your enemy, and love between the sexes is strife. Do not believe either that I gave myself; I did not give, but I took what I wanted. You had one advantage, however, that I realised and wanted you to realise. (II.v, p. 84)

In connection with this statement, if one recalls Laura's earlier questioning of the Law's declaration that the father has the right to decide the future of *his* children, one gets a clue to the driving force behind her ambivalent antagonisms. The law is seen by her as a rational and patriarchal construct that overlooks the law of nature, according to which paternity cannot be conclusively proved, whereas maternity can be. Aligning herself with the laws of nature she asserts the right of matriarchy, which was overthrown to be replaced by patriarchy.[14] Herein lies the root of all sexual conflict. Because the women in their continual efforts to regain their lost power subvert and insidiously undercut all male constructs, they appear as destructive vampires who undermine men. The possibility of a compromise does not exist because one system was completely overthrown to be replaced by the other and thus "one of [them] must go under in this struggle." (II.v, p. 85)

As patriarchy denies women the decision-making powers, she takes her revenge on it by asserting her supremacy and power on the level of personal relationships. As the woman commands the most power in her capacity as mother and nurse, she tends in her relationships with men to view and relate to them on those terms. Her doing so preserves her power and authority, but inevitably gives rise to incestuous suggestions in man-woman relationships. Thus Laura's assertion that the mother was his *friend* is highly ambivalent. Because in the end, it is again a mother surrogate, the nurse, Margaret, who successfully thwarts the Captain's manly assertions and reduces him to the level of a whimpering child, finally symbolically castrating him through the straitjacket. These ambivalences behind the sexual conflict taint all human, familial and social ties.

Furthermore, the sexual conflict transforms the basis of love relationships from one of sharing to one of selfish vampirism. Laura does not give but only takes what she wants, and thus reduces the Captain from an equal partner, to a dispensable agent.

As she says: "Now you have fulfilled your function as an unfortunately necessary father and bread winner. You are not needed any longer and you must go." (II.v, p. 86) Laura, is thus an unconscious vehicle of matriarchal assumptions, a type of "Omphale" (99) who unmans Hercules (i.e. the Captain) by undermining his reason and questioning his virility, by doubting his paternity of Bertha. In this struggle, the Captain is defeated by the "treacherous weakness" of women and dies asserting this fact: "A man has no children, it is only women who have children, and therefore the future is theirs, when we die childless" (III.vii, p. 99).

Though in this conflict Laura appears as a vampire, she is not solely responsible for the destruction of the Captain and their relationship. The Captain is destroyed, both through his persecution complex which is fostered by his monomania and Laura's cruel persecution of him. In the final analysis, the relationship is destroyed because both Laura and the Captain are victims of paradoxical dualities of manly woman and childish man, respectively. The division in their personalities creates the conflict and the division in their relationship, which in turn divides the whole household.[15] This process hints at the manner of proliferation of divisive and destructive forces from the personal to the social level. Essentially solitary and preoccupied with their fragmented selves, the characters cannot create harmonious relationships. Separately they may be good but when they come together, they clash and necessarily "torment the life out of one another." (I.vii, p. 65)

Commenting "on the contradictory systems of his daughter's education in *The Father*, the Cäptain states: "it won't do to try and make a soul in patches like that" (I.iii, p. 54). *Miss Julie*[16] portrays the fate of such a character, possessing a human soul "patched together" out of "torn off samples of Sunday-best clothes that have become rags." (xv) Strindberg's explanation of Miss Julie's tragedy illustrates this, "she is a victim of the discord which a mother's 'crime' implanted in a family; a victim of the errors of her age, of circumstances and of her own flawed constitution." ('Preface,' xvii)

Miss Julie not only locates the source of destructive personal relationships in the split psyche of its characters but it further develops this theme by convincingly relating the conflict between the sexes to the conflict between the classes. Strindberg establishes this connection in his 'Preface' to the play, in which he states that he finds the joy of life in life's cruel and mighty conflicts (xiii); and these for him are the interrelated conflicts between "social ascent and decline, of higher or lower, better or worse, man and woman" (xii). *Miss Julie* is as much about individual persons as it is about the existing hierarchies and conflict thereof between the genders and social classes. Julie and Jean are individuals in their own right but they also simultaneously represent the affinities and polarities that exist between men and women, the aristocracy and the lower classes. Thus, when Julie the "well favoured individual [goes] under" (xii), it represents the death of her aristocratic family tree and probably the rise of Jean's plebian stock. Strindberg uses the image of the hawk and the flea to further underline the universally predatory motif/ve underlying all these sexual and social relationships or interactions: "The bird of prey eats the dove and the louse eats the bird of prey." (xii) Significantly the categories of dominant and subordinate are not fixed but continually shift and the shifting equations between the predator and prey, oppressor and the victim create the matrix of the play and its action.

The play opens with Julie asserting her right over Jean, her father's servant. Julie snatches Jean away like a predator from Kristin the cook, his fiancé. The opening exchanges between Julie and Jean clearly denote the complex interplay between the sexual and social roles. Julie is attracted toward Jean and is ready to ignore class taboos to dance with him. And yet she is not afraid of rejection because Julie believes that as mistress of the house, she automatically commands Jean's allegiance and that he would unquestioningly obey her orders. Trained to be servile, he would be malleable to be moulded as per her fancy. Julie is a type of Strindberg's modern, confused, half-woman who likes to control her men and breaks gender and class hierarchies. Julie has unsuccessfully tried to 'train' her fiancé and hopes to have better luck with the socially inferior Jean. She tutors him to flirt with her and Jean willingly plays along. Julie actively initiates the flirting with Jean. The gender and class imperatives get mixed as she appropriates a traditionally male prerogative on account of her class superiority. Being a servant, Jean occupies a feminine position in the class hierarchy, but as a male and a natural, sexual aristocrat he attracts Julie and is attracted towards her. He uses his lower class status to his advantage to gain Julie's sympathy and manipulate her. Julie is sexually attracted to Jean because he is not the usual uncouth servant. Jean aspires to be an aristocrat and therefore he apes them and has superficially acquired their refined tastes and mannerisms. Coming from lower class, he is essentially more 'male' than the effeminate aristocratic men like Julie's fiancé. For instance, when Julie orders Jean to flirt with her, he warns her not to 'play with fire.' It is a clear indication that contrary to her belief, her social position does not 'insure' her or warrant sexual superiority or immunity from exploitation. Jean uses her attraction for him to further his ambition to rise up socially. Thus, it becomes possible for Julie the aristocratic hawk to be finally brought down by Jean the servile flea.

Jean succeeds because a part of Julie is already inclined to fall. She tells him, "I have a recurring dream from time to time: I'm on top of a pillar. I'm sitting there, and I see no possible way of getting down. I feel dizzy when I look down but I know I must get down. I haven't got the courage to throw myself. I can't hold on. I long to be able to just fall but I don't fall. I know I won't have any peace until I'm down, no rest until I'm down,

down to the ground. I also know that once I am down I'll want the ground to open and for me to sink, sink." (12-13) Julie's weak, passive and confused self scripts the downfall of her father, family and lover.

Jean on the other hand dreams of rising up, he is a complete contrast to Julie's feminine passivity. He says: "I dream that I am lying underneath a tall tree in a dark forest. . . . I want to plunder the bird's nest up there with the golden eggs. I climb and climb but the trunk is so thick and slippery and it's so far to the first branch. I know that if I could only reach that first branch I could climb up to the top step by step. I haven't reached it yet but I will reach it" (13). He is the opportunist, who will one day be "the founder of a new species . . . with the brutality of a slave and the insensitivity of a tyrant" (xviii). Jean's dream of social climbing has a marked sexual undertone.

The complexities and dichotomies of the Jean-Julie relationship become evident right from the onset of the play. Jean is attracted towards Julie both as a woman and as an aristocrat who is beyond his reach. Though he respectfully refers to her as 'Miss Julie,' he is also aware of her as a fine looking girl with a good pair of shoulders. Thus at Julie's instigation he for a moment regards her as only a woman and flirts with her. But as Jean cannot for long forget his own class and his ambitions to be upwardly mobile, he soon starts to regard her as a member of the aristocracy who could be used to effect his escape from his class. Jean's ambition is most evidently reflected in the veneer of sophisticated manners he has adopted to emulate the aristocracy. As this sophistication does not penetrate into his innermost being, at the core he remains a slave and as such he becomes divided and continually vacillates between these two poles of his personality. His relationship with Julie creates further fragmentation; because he relates to Julie both as a slave and as a sexual aristocrat, he gets torn between his selfish plans and his desire for her.[17] Thus his 'sympathy' for the upper classes and his love-hate relationship with its representative make him destructive and finally cause his downfall.

The sex war has both individual and class implications. In the 'Preface,' (xvi, xvii) Strindberg suggests that the aristocracy has been weakened due to the battle of the sexes and the women's liberation movement which questioned patriarchal and feudal hierarchies. In their battle for supremacy, the women attacked male constructions of gender and society. The women insidiously destroyed their men and such acts by extension weakened the institutions created, constructed and perpetuated for the preservation of the male self or the dominant class. For instance, Julie's mother through her affairs undermines her husband's authority, sexuality, financial security and his paternity. She ignores his paternal control over his child's upbringing and brings up Julie as a boy. Similarly, the Baroness in *The Link* brings up her son as a girl to undermine her husband. Julie is trained to be dominant and assertive. Unlike other women of her class, she has not been schooled in the art of enhancing her femininity to attract men. She has been taught to hate men while paradoxically being schooled to be like a man. Brought up among farm animals Julie is acutely aware of her biological difference and begins to hate it. Thus while her mother teaches her to hate her own essential female self, her father teaches her to hate her gender.

Her parents's strife / conflict contribute to the destruction of the family, the estate and the child Julie. Born of an antagonistic union and brought up in a strife-ridden environment, Julie's psyche is infected with a fragmented and ruptured sense of self. Julie further reflects and replicates the selfish, antagonistic principle in her own sexual and social relationships with the opposite sex. The principle of divisiveness and competitiveness gets further transmitted from the sexual to the social plane. The Jean/ Julie relationship represents the conflation of the sexual struggle for supremacy with the class struggle for ascendancy. The degeneration within Julie's family represents the degeneracy of the dissipated and decrepit aristocracy. Her death marks the end of the Count's family and by extension of the aristocracy which she represents. Julie is destroyed by the contrary pulls of her heredity that is her essential weak female self and her environment of sexual strife between her parents for dominance and supremacy. A product of the man-woman conflict, her split self inheres and perpetuates this principle in her own social and sexual relationships. The female represents all that is weak and it is therefore abhorred by both men and women alike.

The machinations of the vampirish women drain the vitality of the aristocracy and gradually lead to its feminization and a corresponding growth in power and vigour of the lower classes. The fall of one leads to the rise of the 'other.' It also suggests a past when the aristocracy was governed by the 'male' principle. The count represents the positive remnant of that glorious past. The aristocracy that Strindberg portrays in *Miss Julie* is full of 'superannuated trees' (xii) that is decadent, diseased, weak and without a 'Will.' Women according to him are either parasitic, confused, diffused and have no goals, like Julie or they are competitive, vampirish and cannibalistic like her mother. He, therefore, uses Julie to represent a dying aristocracy. In *Miss Julie*, Strindberg reveals a gendered perspective on class. He chooses to represent the positive aspects of a class through the men and the negative aspects through the women. For instance, Kristin the cook is servile, devout and superstitious. She is not assertive or ambitious and occasionally steals too. There is no redeeming feature in her character and she represents the downside of the lower classes. Jean, on the other hand, is ambitious and assertive and represents the survival spirit of his class. He too steals but it is represented as a mark of his cunning intelligence. He is confident of achieving his dream of becoming a count himself.

The Count and Julie's fiancé present the positive 'male' aspect of the aristocracy. Both these characters never appear on stage but are referred to by the other characters. The Count is represented through his boots, which symbolise authority and power and probably are also the reminder of the lost power and glory of the aristocracy i.e. literally on its last leg. The count is the last male member of his house and as he has no male heir his line will die out with him. He represents the residual remnants of a glorious past. Though Julie's fiancé is not able to satisfy her, he represents positive independence of will in refusing to submit to her domination. The men irrespective of class know what they want. The women on the other hand are confused; they are passionate but ineffective. They are easily fooled by the men because they harbour illusory ideas about love. The upper class woman appears to be more confused and deluded because she has been exposed to new ideas of gender equality. The lower class women like Kristin appear to have a more matter-of-fact and practical approach to sexual matters. Julie needs to believe that she is in 'love' with Jean to accept with equanimity her sexual attraction and intimacy with a lower class man. Significantly, Julie does not command the respect that the Count her father does. The servants discuss Julie and her mother but dare not discuss the Count. Even in his absence, he is a strong presence.

The tragedy of their relationship lies in the fact that both are prisoners of their psyche, class and upbringing. Jean cannot escape his class and Julie her discordant upbringing. Jean can never shed his fears and respect for the Count, can never be free of his slave mentality which makes him quake at the sight of the Count's boots. Julie, too, lacks a definite sense of self. Caught in the hatred of her parents's relationship, she is brought up on contradictory lines. Her mother teaches her to hate men, her father, her own sex, and thus she becomes a half woman and half man continually vacillating between the two. As she herself states: "I haven't got a self; I haven't a thought that I don't get from my father, nor an emotion that I don't get from my mother" (44). This duality and vacillation is reflected in her own relationship with Jean where she starts by taking the male's prerogative in love, but after she is seduced, the woman in her feels the shame and she can no longer sustain her supremacy and falls to the level of imploring Jean to *order* her to kill herself. Her shame is also the shame of the aristocrat who feels humiliated by the peasants's victory.

As both Jean and Julie are full of contradictions, their relationship too is unstable. In the beginning, Julie appears as the mistress, but with her seduction she falls to Jean's level, and finally escapes out of this situation and gains ascendancy through her suicide. As no relationship is stable, the sexual and the social differences cannot ever be reconciled. The impossibility of reconciliation is also suggested through their self-centred preoccupations, which make them enter into relationships with selfish motives. These selfish drives so isolate them that they cannot understand each other. Jean's confession to Julie proves as much, "I can see you are unhappy . . . but *I can't understand you*" (32, my italics). Thus they can come together only momentarily, to experience a very brief period of happiness, before the violence erupts and destroys everything. Because the man-woman relationship is based on the vampire motif of taking and not on sharing, it becomes steeped in falsities and hatred and remains necessarily transitory in nature.

The traditional image of an ideal relationship between the sexes and the classes is one based on love, trust and sharing. In *Miss Julie*, hate seems to be the governing force behind these relations. Julie naively believes that her servants love her till Jean disabuses her of her mistaken beliefs: "No, Miss Julie, they don't love you—they eat your food but behind your back they spit at you" (19). Even while Jean warns her against her servants he plans to compromise her by asking her to come into his room. Relationships in *Miss Julie* are all about power, hierarchy, control and exploitation. Men and women use one another to further their whims and ambitions. Romantic love is highly idealised and overrated. It serves the only practical purpose of bringing the two irreconcilable forces of the male and the female briefly together for a momentary union. In his plays, Strindberg lays bare the ugliness and violence that lies underneath the veneer of love. Love is a false emotion that deludes people. For instance, Julie needs to believe in love to accept and condone her sexual transgression. She uses the idea of love to invest a momentary lustful and impulsive act with meaning and escape the shame. For Jean, the concept is a good tool to seduce women and satisfy his sexual urge and male ego. He is a man of the world, well versed in the manipulative rhetoric of love. He blatantly lies to Julie about his childhood fascination and love for her to win her trust and trap her. It is a game he very consciously and calculatingly plays to rise up the social ladder. He confesses as much to Julie. Jean successfully fabricates his tale to feed into Julie's romantic fantasies. The real and 'dirty' nature of his feelings he reveals only after he has had her and Julie has fallen to his level. Julie is unable to accept her sexuality so crassly. She desperately clings to the illusion of love to make the momentary appear as lasting. Jean too plays along for his own self-preservation and social advancement. He is not able to sustain the illusion for long and begins to feel drained by Julie's parasitic dependence on him. He begins to realize the hollowness of the aristocracy. The weak woman and the dying class conflate in the figure of Julie needing the intervention of Jean the strong male and the resurgent class. Jean lives and Julie dies and yet in the final analysis Julie seems to be the winner. The complex nature of these relationships defy easy categorisation. Ultimately there are no winners—the conflict continues with new players.

In such relationships as depicted here, there can be no clear-cut victory. For instance, though Jean seems to have survived because he is the slave and hence stronger, we are made forcefully aware that in giving Julie the razor he has destroyed his own chances of survival. Realizing this, Jean 'turns coward' and refuses to order Julie, to go and kill herself. But as the destruction of each is as inevitable as the conflict, he finally utters the fatal word: "it's terrible—but there's no other way [out] Go . . ." (46). There truly is "no other way out," these basically isolated characters 'cannot combine' but only "collide and damage each other."[18]

The Creditors (1898) again presents a bleak picture of human relationships.[19] All relationships are exposed to be based on ambivalent subterfuges and hence to be basically dangerous. The Tekia-Adolph relation reflects one such ambivalent subterfuge. Though they are husband and wife, they address each other as brother and sister. They apparently do this to preserve the purity of the relationship but this rebounds on them and taints the relation with the suggestions of incest. On the other hand, Gustav, Tekla's former husband, uses the disguise of friendship to revenge himself on Tekla by undermining and finally destroying Adolph. Furthermore, Tekla's relationships with her husbands are exposed to be parasitic and vampiric. In this scenario, friends and friendship appear as destructive agents who insidiously infect and destroy a person's sense of identity. *Creditors* thus presents the negative, soul-destroying aspects of each human relationship.

A Dream Play (1902)[20] in many ways makes explicit the reasons behind the negative drives of human beings. One of the main reasons behind human suffering seems to be the fragmented nature of the universe. This makes each person feel isolated and inadequate because they represent and experience only one aspect of life. Not knowing the totality of human experience makes these characters obsessed with one idea and hence in their relationships with others they cannot understand them, and thus are born relationships full of misunderstandings and strife.[21]

Like other Strindberg characters. Indra's daughter too starts on her experience of human relations with the idealistic notion: "Life is hard—but love conquers all." But she soon comes to experience that "love" which is "the fairest of things" is also the "bitterest" (206). In fact in this world "nothing is as . . . imagined" (197) and thus the "child" which was to be their (the daughter's and the advocate's) "salvation" proves to be their "ruin" (208). The tragedy of human life lies in the fact that one does not have to be guilty to be "contaminated by the petty dirt of life." (219). For instance, the advocate gets contaminated by the crimes of other people.

It is a "curious world of contradictions" (216) and there is no escape from the pain it generates, except through "suffering" which is the only "liberator" (251). The "discord" in the soul created by divided allegiances causes the "small disharmonies" of life which "tear" men and their relationships apart (248). Death represented here through the burning castle and the flowering chrysanthemum, thus, becomes not a symbol of defeat but of a final victory over the discords of life.

The misery of an imperfect world is most effectively presented in *The Ghost Sonata* (1907)[22] through its masked characters, who in their attempts to forget their own realities convert life into an endless masquerade.[23] This attempt creates a highly complicated web of relationships all of which reflect that what appears to be true is not the real truth. For example, Adelé turns out to be not the Colonel's, but Hummel's illegitimate daughter. Thus, in this world of deceptions where nothing reflects the reality, ideals are exposed as masks that try to hide or overlook the reality, of "the dirt of life." The tragic reality of this life is that beauty, like the hyacinths in Adelé's room, can be poisonous. Thus, mankind's attempts to create harmony and beauty inevitably turn to dust; ideals are thwarted and ugliness prevails.

The tragedy of this human situation is reflected in the Mummy's speech: "We're bound together by our sins and a guilty conscience, I suppose. . . . Oh, we've tried dozens of times to split up and to go each his separate way, but, somehow, we're always drawn together again." Furthermore, the self-deceptions of these characters poison the lives of their children and thus infect the very source of life.

The sense of universal contamination and predatoriness is best reflected in Hummel. Himself a cripple, he lives like a vampire, through others, by controlling and appropriating their lives into himself. As he also suggests the experience of age in his relationship with the student, he reflects the parasitic nature of age which feeds on youthful vitality.[24] Furthermore, in his relationship with the vampire cook he is aligned to the lower classes and this reflects the proliferation of the predatory motive from the sphere of personal relationships to the class struggle. As Hummel has also been a vampiric moneylender, his career effectively suggests the tainting of personal, social, class and business relationships. (I.ii, p. 125)

The tragedy of these destructive relationships is that "it is a tragedy that has got into the bloodstream . . . [into] the living process itself." Thus victims of an imperfect world, ravaged by their own ambivalences, these men and women can do nothing but lament: "Oh, God! why aren't we dead? If only we were dead!" (I.ii, p. 119) In their anguished death wish is a cry for deliverance that echoes across Strindberg's canon and reflects his nightmare vision.

Strindberg's plays reflect that all tragic disruptions stem from the conflicting and ambivalent relationships between the sexes. The primary reason behind these disintegrating relationships is the solitary nature of the characters, who most often are divided and maladjusted. To cover up this sense of dislocation, they usually project forth a completely different self from their real one. In its turn this masking of the reality gives rise to relationships that are based on falsities and are hence basically ambivalent. Thus, while by themselves, they might appear as good and whole, their relationship with the opposite sex makes them aware of their hidden ambivalences and they become monstrous. Seething with repressed feelings of violence and indignation, these relationships only need a pretext to burst forth into the full-fledged battle between the sexes. This battle for supremacy and domination has only one inevitable end, that is the destruction of the weaker partner. But as this battle is also the external manifestation of an inner conflict, the destruction of one necessarily leaves the other maimed and incomplete. That it is an ongoing process is best illustrated through the cyclical and repetitive pattern of *The Road to Damascus*.[25] The poisonous effects of this conflict get perpetuated through the children who, to begin with, are innocent victims, but who, in their turn, in their relationships, inevitably poison and contaminate the whole society. It thus proliferates down from the personal level to contaminate all relations and consequently all social transactions reflect destructive motives. Thus, prisoners of their own selves and the world they create, Strindberg's characters can free themselves only through death.

NOTES

1 *August Strindberg: Plays Two*, trans. Michael Meyer (London: Methuen, 1964), p. 250.

2 "August Strindberg," *Modern Drama: Essays in Criticism*, ed. Travis Bogard and William Oliver (New York: Oxford University Press, 1965), pp. 320-21.

3 See Maurice Valency, *The Flower and the Castle: An Introduction to Modern Drama* (New York: Macmillan, 1963), p. 244 in which he states that "the study of Strindberg is inevitably a study in biography."

4 August Strindberg, *The Road to Damascus: A Trilogy*, trans. Graham Rawson (1939; rpt. London: Jonathan Cape, 1968).

5 August Strindberg, *The Ghost Sonata*, trans. Max Faber in *August Strindberg: Miss Julie and Other Plays*, ed. & intro. John Allen (London: Heinemann, 1960), p. 103.

6 August Strindberg, *The Link: A Tragedy in One Act*, trans. Edwin Bjorkman, *Eight Best Plays: August Strindberg*, ed. & intro. Alan Harris (1949; rpt. Surrey: The Gresham Press, 1979).

7 Strindberg in *The Father* and *Creditors* had suggested that sexual love is riddled with incestuous drives.

8 The prototypes of the Baroness can be seen in the characters of Laura in *The Father*, Julie's Mother in *Miss Julie* and Tekia in *Creditors*—all of whom try to unman their men.

9 The motif of imprisonment and self-destruction appears in both the naturalistic and the dream plays.

10 August Strindberg, *The Father: A Tragedy*, trans. N. Erichson in *Eight Best Plays: August Strindberg*, ed. & intro. Alan Harris (1949; rpt. Surrey: The Gresham Press, 1979).

11 Raymond Williams, "Strindberg and Modern Tragedy," *Essays on Strindberg*, ed. Carl Reinhold Smedmark (Stockholm: J. Beckmans, Bokfôrlag, 1966), p. 8.

12 A similar motive drives the Stranger in *To Damascus* to seek his completion and salvation through the Lady, who also represents all womanhood, the mother, mistress etc.

13 Maurice Valency, *The Flower and the Castle*, p. 270.

14 Martin Lamm, "August Strindberg," *Modern Drama*, trans. Karin Elliot (Oxford: Basil Blackwell, 1952), p. 138 states that in 1886 Strindberg had read a newspaper article by Paul Lafargue which contained the description of the battle of the sexes that preceded the introduction of patriarchy. Strindberg's awareness of the subject is reflected in Laura's unconscious drives.

15 The Captain's household in *The Father* gets divided with all the women grouping together against him.

16 August Strindberg, *Miss Julie: A Naturalistic Tragedy including Strindberg's Preface to the Play*, trans. & Intro. Helen Cooper (London Methuen, 1992).

17 Martin Lamm, "Miss Julie," trans. & abr. Otto Reinert from *Strindberg's Dreamer* (Stockholm: Albert Bonniers Forlag, 1924), vol. 1, rpt. in *Strindberg: A Collection of Critical Essays*, ed. Otto Reinert (Englewood Cliffs, N.J.: Prentice Hall, 1971), p. 111.

18 Raymond Williams, "Strindberg and Modern Tragedy," p. 11.

19 August Strindberg, *Creditors*, trans. Max Faber, in *Strindberg: Miss Julie & Other Plays*.

20 August Strindberg, *A Dream Play*, in *August Strindberg Plays: Two*.

21 As these characters also represent the contrary aspects of a personality they suggest the source of all conflict to arise out of man's conflicting desires.

22 August Strindberg, *The Ghost Sonata*, trans. Max Faber, in *Strindberg: Miss Julie and Other Plays*.

23 In this they resemble the quarantine Master of *A Dream Play*, who goes to masquerades to forget himself.

24 J.R. Northam, "Strindberg's *Spook Sonata*," *Essays on Strindberg*, ed. Carl Reinhold Smedmark, p. 41.

25 Raymond Williams, "Strindberg and Modern Tragedy," p.13.

Bibliography

Allen, John. *Masters of European Drama*. London: Dennis Dobson, 1962.

Bellquist, John Eric. "Strindberg's *Father*: Symbolism, Nihilism, Myth," *Modern Drama*, XXIX (December 1986), 532-43.

Bentley, Eric. *The Playwright as Thinker: A Study of Drama in Modern Times*. 1946; rpt. New York: Meridian Books, 1960.

Brustein, Robert. "Male and Female in August Strindberg." *Modern Drama: Essays in Criticism*. Ed. Travis Bogard and William Oliver. New York: Oxford University Press, 1965.

Freedman, Morris, "Strindberg's Positive Nihilism." *Essays in Modern Drama*. Ed. Morris Freedman. Boston: D.C. Heath, 1964.

Gassner, John. *The Theatre in Our Times*. New York: Crown, 1954.

Lamm, Martin. *Modern Drama*. Trans. Karin Elliot. Oxford: Basil Blackwell,1952.

_____. "Strindberg and the Theatre." Trans. Thomas R. Buckman, *The Tulane Drama Review*, VI, No. 2 (November 1961-62), 132-39.

Lucas, F.L. *The Drama of Ibsen and Strindberg*. London: Cassell, 1962.

Modern Drama, V (December 1962) Strindberg issue, ed. Robert Shedd.

Parker, Gerald. "The Spectator Seized by the Theatre: Strindberg's *The Ghost Sonata*." *Modern Drama*, XIV(February 1972), 373-86.

Reinert, Otto, ed. *Strindberg: A Collection of Critical Essays*, Twentieth Century Views. Englewood Cliffs, N.J.: Prentice Hall, 1971.

Scobbie, Irene. "Strindberg and Lagerkvi." *Modern Drama*. VII (September 1962), 126-34.

Smedmark, Carl Reinhold, ed. *Essays on Strindberg*, Stockholm: Beckmans Bokfôrlag, 1966.

Styan, J.L. *The Dark Comedy*. Cambridge: Cambridge University Press, 1968.

_____. *Modern Drama in Theory and Practice*. Vols. I & II. Cambridge: Cambridge University Press, 1981.

Valency, Maurice. *The Flower and the Castle*. New York: Macmillan, 1963.

Williams, Raymond. *Drama from Ibsen to Eliot*. London: Chatto & Windus, l954.

_____. *Modern Tragedy*. London: Chatto & Windus, 1966.

